‖‖‖‖‖‖‖‖‖‖‖‖‖‖‖‖‖‖‖‖‖‖‖‖‖‖

P9-APR-761

EMBERS OF THE WORLD

CONVERSATIONS WITH SCOTT BUCHANAN

Participants:
Harris Wofford, Jr.
Stringfellow Barr
Jacqueline Grennan
Roger Landrum
and
David Schickele

EDITED BY HARRIS WOFFORD, JR.

PUBLISHED BY
THE CENTER FOR THE STUDY OF DEMOCRATIC INSTITUTIONS
SANTA BARBARA, CALIFORNIA

SCOTT BUCHANAN
(1895-1968)

When I invited Scott Buchanan to join the staff of the Fund for the Republic, he asked what I wanted him to do.

I said, "Teach us."

This he proceeded, unobtrusively, to do.

He was one of the great teachers of our time. If any member of the Center were asked who the important influences in his life had been he would include Scott Buchanan in the list.

He was an unusual combination of wisdom and imagination. He was the first person ever to mention the significance of developing countries in my hearing. He was the first to talk about what technology had done and would do to civilization. He was the first to propose a positive interpretation of the Bill of Rights and to put forward the idea that the First Amendment imposed obligations on the government to support and advance the enlightenment of the people. We are all glad that we were able to get his discussion of the Constitution into print before his death.

He symbolized for us what we were trying to be and do. He personified the Civilization of the Dialogue.

ROBERT M. HUTCHINS

INTRODUCTION

Scott Buchanan will always be Socrates for me, and for many others.

"Stick as close to Scott Buchanan and Stringfellow Barr as you can," Robert Hutchins advised me in 1945. Just back from the Air Force, I was trying to decide whether to go to the University of Chicago, where Hutchins presided as chancellor, or to St. John's College, where Buchanan and Barr had introduced the full four-year Great Books program Chicago was only partly following. "Go to St. John's and get the whole thing," Hutchins urged.

So I went down to Annapolis and met Scott Buchanan. He was the dean of the college and author of the New Program begun there in 1937. I told him that his Catalog (reprinted in part at the end of this book) seemed to offer the hardest but best curriculum available. He looked me in the eye and asked, "Are you the sort of fellow who says that and then doesn't have the courage to come here?"

I was. For better and worse, I chose Chicago's short-form, and ever since I have been trying to make up for the books, the foreign languages and the mathematics I missed at St. John's.

It was my good fortune to encounter Buchanan many times in the next twenty-three years. Though I never took a course from him or saw him in a classroom he became the one who comes to my mind when I hear the word "teacher."

When I learned that Scott Buchanan was dying, I armed myself with a tape recorder and went to Santa

Barbara to try to catch some of his last reflections and questions. My notion of a recorded oral autobiography embarrassed him, but he came to enjoy doing it, usually absorbing my questions into a more general conversation that kept circling around his central themes; whenever I touched a personal button, an idea came back.

The first of these conversations took place in August 1966; the last one was on his 73rd birthday in March 1968. "I think that's it," he said. Eight days later he died.

Is it possible to capture such a teacher in cold print? Not wholly; these abridged and edited dialogues are second-best Buchanan, hardly conveying his irony or gaiety, doing less than justice to the great guffaw, the real laugh, with which he greeted the "funny stuff" he found everywhere.

"Scott Buchanan is the one man in the world whom I simultaneously love and fear," said Mark Van Doren in 1958 on the 21st anniversary of the St. John's program. Van Doren called that program "an act of creation that has no parallel in our time." But he had come to talk of the man who made it—one "who believes the truth must be found and yet may not be found, who had the greatest and purest influence on me." Buchanan, he said, was an incendiary who "burns slowly and smokelessly." The other incendiary he toasted that day, Stringfellow Barr, president of St. John's from 1937 to 1947, he saw as one who "burns with a blaze, bright and red and always there." The red-headed, articulate Virginian, "Winkie" Barr, in this book gives his own account of how he collided with Buchanan at Oxford and never recovered.

Let me cite one other witness to the spell Buchanan cast over so many of those who knew him. Clifton Fadiman dedicated his book *Fantasia Mathematica* to *"Scott Buchanan, Mover of Minds, Who Started This."*

Fadiman called him "one of the most remarkable men I have ever met," and went on to say:

> I should like some day to write at length about him. He is the only distinguished representative I know of a species practically extinct, or in any case obsolescent—the vagabond intellectual. . . . Though he is a philosopher by training, his real interest is simply in thought, thought in almost any area. Wherever intellectual curiosity has led him, there he has strayed, as reveler or as ponderer.

Buchanan also has been called a destroyer, an irresponsible amateur, and a corrupter of young men—a man who drew students into worlds of the intellect too difficult for them, who made them, as Buchanan concedes in these conversations, "misfits in the universe for the time being."

He himself had much personal experience with the role of misfit—in Vermont, at Oxford, at Harvard, at Virginia, at Chicago, in the Progressive Party, in the World Government movement, in Israel, at the Center for the Study of Democratic Institutions at Santa Barbara, in American politics and academia generally. Except for his smallest book, *Poetry and Mathematics,* and his introduction to Viking's *Portable Plato,* his writings have not been widely read. His doctoral thesis, *Possibility,* his book on the liberal arts and the art of medicine, *The Doctrine of Signatures,* and his major political work, *Essay in Politics,* are out of print.

Most of his enterprises went awry, or at least fell short of his expectations. Certainly the war against the elective system which Hutchins, Van Doren, Barr and Buchanan mounted in the thirties has not been won; if anything, most current notions of curricular reform would compound the anarchy of the multiversity. Long before it was coined, the student slogan, "let everyone do his thing," was the governing principle of most departments and most professors in most colleges; and it is surely the opposite of the search for a common curriculum of liberal arts for all citizens Buchanan wrote about in the St. John's College Catalog.

So, as the world goes, he was hardly a success, denied fame, power or large influence; and he himself denies that he was a tragic hero. Why then did it seem so important to record and publish these conversations? Why is it that countless students and friends speak of Scott Buchanan as the drunken Alcibiades did of Socrates at the end of the *Symposium*?

> When we listen to any one else talking, however eloquent he is, we don't really care a damn what he says; but when we listen to you, or to someone else repeating what you've said, even if he puts it ever so badly, we're absolutely staggered and bewitched. And speaking for myself, gentlemen, if I wasn't afraid you'd tell me I was completely bottled, I'd swear an oath what an extraordinary effect his words have had on me—and still do. For the moment I hear him speak I am smitten by a kind of sacred rage—oh, and not only me, but lots of other men. Yes, I have heard Pericles and all the other great orators, but they never affected me like that; they never turned my whole soul upside down . . . I've been bitten by something much more poisonous than a snake; in fact, mine is the most painful kind of bite there is. I've been bitten in the heart, or the mind, or whatever you like to call it.

Perhaps it is because Buchanan so regularly and unapologetically spoke of the heart and the mind and the soul, and so few other people do. Even now in the midst of a conversation the talk, including my own, will suddenly seem insufferably dull. Buchanan could take the most trivial point, his own as well as others, and in quick jumps carry the conversation to an important plane. He treated almost any statement as a question to be entertained and followed. He did believe, as he was once accused of believing, that a sentence understood is more intimate than a kiss. He claimed to know little—to have no doctrines for sale—but he was always discovering something interesting.

I remember his delight in reading Sir Frederick Maitland's almost Homeric list of the corporate ships that make up modern civilization, from the medieval church and monastery to the universities, townships and guilds, to the early trading companies that became colonies, to the modern business corporation, trusts, trade unions, and nation states. The intellectual ships sailing back and forth in Buchanan's mind as he searched for an idea of the world make quite a suggestive list too, and most of them are here in this book.

Buchanan talked of men being engaged in dialogue with law, history, truth, and God; and it was his gift to bring that dialogue to life for those talking with him. He listened with a curiosity that said: "You are going to have something important to say, if not just now, then next time we talk."

The Scott Buchanan we knew had the strength of a long-distance runner and the gentleness of the brooding teacher he describes. Now he is like a faraway mountain, no longer at hand, but ever in the corner of our eyes. Fortunately, some of his words remain.

The 1952 commencement talk, *Imago Mundi,* at the end of this book, was given on a gray day under the historic great tree in Annapolis while thunder threatened rain. I hear him still, speaking as "an old man of the tribe," telling the young men that they were beautiful and strong, but reminding them that what was being celebrated was not youth but the world. The systems and ideologies in our firmament are "but hypotheses," he said. "For all their heroic dimensions, they are merely possibilities, which with boldness, laughter and ingenuity on our part can be put aside and replaced."

The 1958 anniversary talk, which opens this book, was given on another May day, this time in bright sun on a lawn by the Hudson River. Here he was responding to the testimonials and toasts of sixty or seventy of his students and friends. "When I run into a St. Johnnie or two, in no time at all a conversation springs up, like fresh water from an old spring, in a world where there are fewer and fewer conversations," he began.

Ten years later, when I came to Santa Barbara to record these conversations, I was drawing on the old spring to quench my own thirst. Scott knew he was dying, and that I knew it too, and he laughed at the Socratic twist: he, too, was atrophying from his legs up. After repeated aneurisms and operations on the arteries of his legs he needed to keep walking around, like Socrates taking the hemlock, in order to keep his circulation going.

Most of our talks took place in the living room of his modest house in Montecito, with him sitting, as was his custom, with his back to the window and its view of the valley and mountains. Dürer's drawing, *Melancholia,* was on the wall and the shelves were full of well-worn books. Scott's wife, Miriam, listened on the edge of the conversation, as she had done for nearly fifty years since they met in a small New England town. She, too, died within the year.

On one occasion we were joined by three friends who were helping me plan a new college of the State University of New York at Old Westbury: Jacqueline Grennan, then a nun and president of Webster College, already beginning to secularize herself and her college; Roger Landrum, former Peace Corps teacher at the University of Nigeria, then about to organize a new agency for teacher-training and inner-city volunteer teaching called "Teachers, Inc."; and David Schickele, former Volunteer from the University of Nigeria, then starting on his career as film-maker. In the fifth of the conversations they replace me when I was called away.

There were seven conversations in all, separated by as much as six months. Both Scott and I repeated ourselves, and the repetition is significant. The same major themes keep recurring, sometimes arising in new forms to be examined from new angles, but in any guise endlessly complicated and endlessly interesting to him (and to me). Scott Buchanan never let the world get all flattened out.

Those who knew Buchanan well will find little new here—except perhaps the surprising weight he gives to his pre-Oxford purpose to spend the rest of his life in India; his dream of being Woodrow Wilson's man Friday; and the discussion of religion. The two subjects he had wanted to write his thesis on at Harvard—Tragedy and Authority—were vetoed by the Philosophy Department and he never got around to writing much about these. My tape recorder exercised no such censorship. And the title he originally chose for his *Essay on Politics,* which his publisher vetoed, also can be said to have been revived here as descriptive of one of his overall themes about modern man: *The Withering of Consent.*

On the evening before he sailed for Oxford after World War I, Scott said: "I am going to view the embers of the world." He spent the rest of his life trying to view the world, steady and whole, somewhere between ashes and Phoenix-like reconstruction. The results must be rated as fragmentary, but for some of us he brought the world into focus, at least for a time, and his ideas and words glow like embers.

HARRIS WOFFORD, JR.

Old Westbury, New York
December, 1969

CONTENTS

A TALK TO FRIENDS

*Excerpts from remarks by Scott Buchanan,
May 31, 1958, on the 21st anniversary of the
New Program at St. John's College*

How are you doing? Do you believe in and trust your
intellect, that innate power that never sleeps? Do you
recognize the action of this power as you live and learn?
You have lived a lot. You have fallen into the hands
of scholars and into the grooves of practice. You have
suffered the winds of doctrine and have gotten lost in
the jungle of ideologies. Latterly you have been stormed
by scientific miracle and guess. In all these learnings
and practices have you listened to the small spontaneous
voice within that asks continually if these things are
true? Have you allowed this voice to speak louder and
remind you that you do not know, that you know you
do not know, that you know what you do not know?
Do you believe that knowledge is possible, that truth
is attainable, and that it is always your business to seek
it, although evidence is overwhelmingly against it?

Have you in the course of your life, before, after,
or while you were at St. John's, become your own
teacher? Have you yet recognized that you are and
always have been your own teacher? Liberal education
has as its end the free mind, and the free mind must

be its own teacher. Intellectual freedom begins when one says with Socrates that he knows nothing, and then goes on to add: I know what it is that I don't know. My question then is: Do you know what you don't know and therefore what you should know? If your answer is affirmative and humble, then you are your own teacher, you are making your own assignment, and you will be your own best critic.

My next question is different from the first two, more superficial perhaps, but fateful, nevertheless. Under the slings and arrows of outrageous fortune, have you persuaded yourself that there are knowledges and truths beyond your grasp, things that you simply cannot learn? Have you allowed adverse evidence to pile up and force you to conclude that you are not mathematical, not linguistic, not poetic, not scientific, not philosophical? If you have allowed this to happen, you have arbitrarily imposed limits on your intellectual freedom and you have smothered the fires from which all other freedoms arise.

Most of us have done this and come short of what that threadbare slogan, human dignity, really means. We are willing, and shamefully relieved, to admit that each has his specialty, his so-called field, and the other fellow has his, and we are ready to let the common human enterprise go by default. We are willing to become cripples in our minds and fractions of men in our lives. Some of us are willing to crush the Socratic formula and say, I *know* nothing.

The last question: Do you accept the world? In *The Brothers Karamazov,* Ivan tells Alyosha that he finds it easy to believe in God, but that he finds it impossible to believe in the world. For most of us these days, we have believed in some things so weakly or fanatically that other equally or more real things have become absurd or impossible. This results from our crippled minds, our self-imposed limits on understanding, our deafness to the voice that asks: Is it true? I am persuaded that the cure for this sickness of mind is in some vigorous and rigorous attempt to deal with that most puzzling and mysterious idea, the idea of the world. It is not a simple idea, nor even a merely complicated idea. Kant called it an antinomy, an idea of speculative reason governing all other uses of the intellect. There have been other such ideas that have governed thought, the idea of God or Being as it puzzled and dazzled the ancient world, the idea of Man as it stirred and fermented the world from the Renaissance on. God and Man have not disappeared as charts and aids to intellectual navigation, but they are in partial eclipse at present, and the world is asking us the big questions, questions in cosmology and science, questions in law and government. They are not merely speculative questions; they are concrete and immediately practical. They are as much matters of life and death and freedom as the old questions were. Most of us have made, with Ivan, a pact with the devil, an agreement not to face them and accept them—yet.

I

THE
SOCRATIC PROCESS
[August 28, 1966]

Socrates or Jesus?

HARRIS WOFFORD: Over the years I've heard your students say you make them think of Socrates, and your critics say you've been unduly fascinated by the Socratic model. When did you first come across him?

SCOTT BUCHANAN: As far as I remember, there was a very early debate in school—way, way back—whether Socrates or Jesus was more important.

WOFFORD: Where and when was this?

BUCHANAN: Back in Jeffersonville, Vermont, in some grammar school reader in the early 1900's, but that didn't make much impression on me. It was done on the basis of reading history, not Plato. The first time I ran into Socrates head on was as a freshman at Amherst. I had done two years of Greek in high school, and it was a natural thing to continue with it. The freshman class in Greek was reading the *Apology* in the old fashioned method of studying the classics: so many lines a day, and you better be sure you knew the grammar and could answer questions on constructions. It didn't make much difference whether you understood what was being said. But once in a while the teacher we had, a serious old fellow, would sit back and talk about what the text was saying. He obviously very much admired Socrates. He'd point to the famous bust of Socrates in the back of the room, and say, "You see that fellow over there, that ugly head," and then he'd talk about him. I was impressed, but not any more than I would have been if he'd been talking about Achilles. Then I went on with a much better professor in Greek and read the *Phaedo* and a couple of other dialogues, but not the *Republic*. This professor referred to the *Republic* as the Great Book you'd want to get to some time. Of course we were reading other things like the Tragedies and some of the Comedies, Aristophanes and Sophocles.

But I never really got to Plato until much later—in New York in the late '20's when I was Assistant Director of the People's Institute. Several people who went to the big lectures in Cooper Union Hall got acquainted with each other and with me and we wanted to read Plato. We met in a famous restaurant on 2nd Avenue opposite the old Jewish Theatre; on Saturday nights' they'd give us a little hole-in-the-wall in back, and we would sit there for four, five, six hours sometimes, discussing Plato. This went on all winter and we did all of Plato. That was really the first experience I had with the sweep of the whole thing.

WOFFORD: Were you already stung before?

BUCHANAN: Yes. The serious work I'd done in philosophy before that was Kant, the three critiques. Oh, I've forgotten one other experience when I did read a good deal of Plato. After I graduated from Amherst and was around the college, one year as Christian Association Secretary and one year as instructor in Greek, there was a senior seminar in Plato. I joined that and read along. And I guess that was the first substantial thing.

Of course, there was another sort of contagion involved. Alec Meiklejohn was the President of Amherst during this time. He talked about Socrates a good deal, and we all recognized that he was really Socratic. He was a great leader of discussion, asking questions of not merely students, but anyone he came in contact with. We used to imagine what happened after the Sunday church service when he'd take the preacher home to lunch with him. We wondered what happened to the sermon at lunch, because Alec never left anything like that alone. He would have questioned the man as he did everybody. This got pretty widespread in the faculty. There were a great many classes done as seminars with questions rather than lectures as the leading point. So, in a sense, it was through Alec Meiklejohn that the whole living Socratic method became clear. There was a time when the whole college seemed to be Socratic. We played Socratic games with each other as students. This wasn't studying Plato; it was practicing the method without knowing it.

WOFFORD: One of the things you do to many of us, is make us feel how badly educated we are. It sounds as if you were fairly well educated. Was it Amherst that led you into an intellectual life, or were you already on your way?

BUCHANAN: No, I don't believe I was on my way, although I certainly had more intellectual interests than most people had in high school. Even back in Vermont where I went to primary school I had read fairly important things by myself—just as they happened to fall out, but not many.

WOFFORD: Happened to fall off your parents' shelves?

BUCHANAN: Or some friend of mine would tell me about something. But when I went to college, compared with my equals there, I felt that I was not well read

7

at all. I feel now that my education has been very bad—very lean and in a funny sense narrow, compared with a good European education. My background in Vermont was like most places in the United States at that time: books were rarities, you didn't have big book shelves in your home. We had some, and there were libraries—two libraries in town—and my parents were both readers, but I never got going very much. I read Alger and all the Green Mountain Boys, funny juvenile novels. My best reading was an extraordinary magazine called *The Youth's Companion*. Along with some original writing it carried several columns of excerpts from great books. This was fascinating. In college I began doing more than most people in reading outside of assignments, including some great books. I remember one summer I had a job in a boat club on a lake; it had an old library with Dante's *Divine Comedy* on the shelf in translation which I read with considerable interest and a great deal of puzzlement. It was a very funny thing; it was beyond me, but I was involved in it very deeply. I made quite a splash when I went back to college and the professor asked a rather large class if anyone had ever read Dante, and I was the only one who raised his hand. But I shouldn't say I was well-educated, and I still feel that I'm not.

WOFFORD: Explain the leanness, the narrowness.

BUCHANAN: I'm reminded of this when we hear now about Headstart. The way you live in your home, the amount of conversation that goes on in your family, the friends that you have, what they're interested in, the kind of domestic culture that you're surrounded with—determines a great deal how much school means to you. Although my family was rather superior in this respect, the surroundings in Vermont were not intellectual at all. Communications were not complicated or subtle or anything of that sort. Awfully good people, humorous and gossipy; a certain kind of ordinary, country-kind of subtlety, if you like; but nothing like a city would provide. I didn't live in a city until I was about 13 years old, and then wasn't a part of it really. So college was the first time I was in a community in which real conversation went on, and college, God knows, is not too good either.

WOFFORD: Schools and books mean so little to most people in this country. I've sensed this among volunteers in the Peace Corps. So many of them say that school never seemed good, books never seemed important. We have ten million students turned off and they never get turned on.

BUCHANAN: That's true. That's what I'm referring to about myself, really. At some point, I don't know when, probably along toward the end of college, I began to recognize deep intellectual interests that would carry on the rest of my life. I was going through the rigmarole before this, with considerable excitement, I must say, but it was not intrinsic. Alec Meiklejohn had a lot to do with this turn, and some other teachers at Amherst. Alec had brought about five people to Amherst and there were some good ones already there—Stark Young, Walter Stewart, Walton Hamilton—and something happened there.

WOFFORD: This was in World War I?

BUCHANAN: I was there from 1912 to 1916 as an undergraduate, so the World War started right in the middle. I began reading *The New York Times*. The whole European complex was a world I'd never heard of before. I'd done my history in school, but this was my real initiation.

WOFFORD: The relevance of books and your turning on to this world had something to do with the fact that great issues were alive then, because World War I was going on?

BUCHANAN: You're right. Because of the war I began, somehow, to penetrate into another level of existence. I was troubled by the whole thing before we got into it, and by the time we got into it I was a conscientious objector. I'd never known I was before. This all developed in a curious way. I was a great church-goer when I was young. Back in Jeffersonville, Vermont, we went to a church my father had something to do with founding. I used to count five times on Sunday that I did something at the church. One was the ordinary church service, and there was the Sunday School, then there was an afternoon meeting, and the Christian Endeavor for young people, and finally there was an evening service where I used to sit with the men and sing.

WOFFORD: What was the church?

BUCHANAN: The Congregational Church, a little bit of a thing, the only church in town. We had no Catholics in town. But this church thing was always interesting and important. I must have got some sort of primitive Christianity that led me into the pacifist thing.

WOFFORD: What did you do after you graduated?

BUCHANAN: I was the Christian Association secretary during 1917 when we entered the war. For another year I went on teaching Greek at the college. Then a very peculiar thing happened. As a conscientious objector I looked into the consequences and thought Ft. Leavenworth was my destination—Leavenworth prison. But they didn't call me up; I'd been exempted because my mother was depending on me. This was a crisis in my life. When you're a conscientious objector and don't get drafted, who are you? I got kind of dialectical about this with myself. Finally a sort of revolutionary thing happened in my mind. A good many of my college mates had been drafted, some of them had been abroad fighting, some of them with the Canadian forces before we were in the war. And then the poem about Flanders

Fields came out. You know, "In Flanders Fields the poppies blow . . ." This knocked me out in some funny, patriotic way. And I said, "What right have I to escape this?" I didn't want to fight, but why should I escape what they were going through in the trenches? So in 1918 I signed up for the Navy, still a pacifist, still a conscientious objector, but feeling that I could not escape. So I was in the Naval Reserve Force training first at Bumpkin Island off Boston, then at Harvard.

Feeling very strung-up and criss-crossed I did something kind of Socratic or Gandhi-ish. I don't think I knew anything about Gandhi, but I was acting that way. I went to the Officer of the Day and said I wanted to be put on report for disrespect to a superior officer. On the list of sins—violations—this had the highest penalty, 40 black points as I remember. He said, "Where and when have you been disrespectful?" I said, "Here and now to you." He said, "How's that?" And I tried to explain that this was how I felt about the whole thing.

I was called to the Commanding Officer and questioned: "Are you Red or are you crazy?" The old captain sent me to the medical officer to find out if I was sane. Finally they sent me to the one Annapolis-trained officer, a very good man, the best teacher we had there, a mathematician, and he said, "You're making things very difficult for us. You're a Christian. Don't you think you ought to stop this kind of protest?" I said, "No, I don't think so," and he said, "I know what you're protesting about. We're all pretty incompetent. You say you think I'm better than most of them but I'm not too competent either and we're having a bad time. This is a war." Then they let me know what the possibilities were: a court of inquiry, dishonorable discharge, loss of citizenship and all sorts of things. And I said, "That's what I want." After that they left me alone for about three weeks. Finally one day I went in to the Commanding Officer and said, "Let's call it off," and he sort of fell on my neck—very happy.

WOFFORD: What *were* you protesting?

BUCHANAN: I think it was my pacifism; and it *was* a very incompetent school. Here we were being trained for what were supposed to be very tough jobs on destroyers, and we weren't learning enough to be competent officers at all. I don't think we were frightened, just sort of angry at the school for this kind of incompetence, and a lot of showoff military playhouse stuff.

I know I read several great books during those months—*War and Peace* for the first time. In the middle of this training Armistice Day came, and we were let out as ensigns. When they gave me my diploma they didn't give it to me with the rest of the class, they called me up on the platform. I guess this was to show that my protest hadn't come to much and I had made terms with them. I'm not very proud of this.

WOFFORD: In deciding to go in, you weighed the desire not to escape against the principle of pacifism?

BUCHANAN: Yes. The question was, supposing you're a pacifist and really serious about it, how do you protest? I thought conscientious objection was the important thing but there was no consequence to that. I thought you had to do something more about it. It's a very curious kind of dialectic that I probably couldn't repeat now.

WOFFORD: At this period was the Christian creed clear and simple for you?

BUCHANAN: No. That's another side of this. I was having trouble religiously, too, all this time.

WOFFORD: Had you started strong and devout, while you were singing in church?

BUCHANAN: This is a funny experience. I don't know whether we ought to be talking about it. I guess it has something to do with the Socratic business. My father died when I was seven years old and left my mother and me alone with hardly any money. My mother was a very stout girl and became a milliner and dressmaker and tried to make her way. She wasn't trained in any real job. But we went on in this little town in Vermont. And an evangelist came by who was very eloquent—a good deal like Billy Graham but on a small scale—and I was converted. I don't know quite what happened but I hit the sawdust trail as an eight-year-old child, about 1903. And they took me in as a member of the church at the age of eight. I don't think this is often done but Congregationalists are free-wheeling and this was a matter of local decision. Then after that I began having doubts, of course, almost right away. I remember I couldn't really understand the Communion Service. And this disturbed me a good deal. By the time I was in high school and went to Massachusetts to live in Worcester, I refused to take Communion. I didn't know what it meant. And this went on for quite some time. I've been interested in theology ever since.

WOFFORD: Your refusal was on what grounds?

BUCHANAN: Just not understanding it. I didn't understand why you should eat bread and drink wine because it was the body and blood of Christ. This seemed to be gobbledygook.

WOFFORD: What was your view of Christ?

BUCHANAN: Pretty straight as a child. I would have believed in the divinity of Christ without any question. I believed the story in the New Testament fully, and knew it well.

WOFFORD: When did the questions come?

BUCHANAN: They came with these funny observances. In the Congregational Church they are pretty empty, you know. The ordinary minister or the ordinary church member couldn't explain them to me. They had never heard of the Eucharist. Soon I got to Massachusetts where there were Catholic churches around, and I used to go to the Catholic Church and wonder what that was all about with great interest.

WOFFORD: Did the doubts lead to Christ getting displaced by Socrates?

BUCHANAN: We had discussion groups in college under the Y.M.C.A. That was the reason I was in the Christian Association. By that time I was pretty skeptical. There was an occasion when the two travelling national secretaries of the Christian Association came to Amherst and told us that they had twenty-seven colleges in the Middle West praying for Amherst because of our secretaryship—because I was so skeptical. I was leading discussion groups then on the Hebrew Prophets, but I was skeptical about the whole Christian thing, and those discussions seemed to be important no matter how they came out. We already had learned that you follow the argument wherever it leads. Sometimes it led to places where you didn't know where you were. Ever since I've had religious problems. I stopped going to church while I was in college and I haven't been back very much. What bothered me weren't the main doctrines, because I didn't know what they were. Chiefly I resented the Church during the war. The church was defending our part in the war, and I couldn't understand how a Christian church could be doing this. I said if I went back to church it would be either as a Quaker or as a Catholic. Both of those made sense, but the Congregational Church or anything in between didn't seem to be honest. It didn't know what it was doing.

WOFFORD: Are you saying you are not a Christian in the same way you say you have never been a Platonist?

BUCHANAN: No, I think I'm pretty deeply Christian. After I finished at Harvard and was in New York, the Dominican translation of Thomas Aquinas' *Summa* came out and for the first time in my life I knew what the Christian doctrine was. I was terribly impressed and felt very deeply involved, with a deep belief in the Christian doctrine. In some deep way I think that's still true with me. I'm not a good Thomist. I'd have great difficulty joining a church—even the Catholic Church horrified me—although I was saying to someone the other day I wish the Ecumenical Councils had come earlier in my life.

WOFFORD: Do you see God and Christ and the Incarnation as facts as well as questions?

BUCHANAN: "Fact" is a funny word to use—but as true, yes, they are a true doctrine. You can ask me, then, why not accept all the rest? I still have difficulty about the church as an institution—and it's heartening to know that even the Roman Church feels this way now.

WOFFORD: Could you explain the understanding Aquinas gave you?

BUCHANAN: That would be long and difficult. The Incarnation, of course, is the center of the doctrine—it's the great doctrine. This can be arrived at by a good many different routes. I don't think Plato taught a doctrine but there are insights which make the Incarnation almost a necessity as far as I'm concerned. It's difficult to expound; I'd have to prepare it; I haven't been doing it for quite a long time in any systematic way. Once I gave a lecture on this at the University of Virginia and presented one of the accounts of the Incarnation that seemed impressive—not an orthodox but a philosophical approach. Ideas—universal abstract ideas in the Platonic sense—have to be embodied. It may take all of history and more to do this, but history is doing this all the time. And if you look at it as a whole big system of ideas there must be at the top of this *the* idea. The One, the Good, the Universal, the True, and so forth— these are called transcendental terms and have a very peculiar relationship with each other. These ideas also have to be embodied, and the center of this whole thing would be an idea of God which has to be realized in existence. This is what some Protestants talk about as the entrance of God into history as Christ. This is what we celebrate at Christmas and what the Eucharist is all about, and all the rest flows from this.

My early concern about the Communion made me read the treatises on the Sacraments at the end of the *Summa* with deep interest. Several of us were reading the *Summa* in the 1930's as the Dominican translation came out over a period of about ten years. You read the first part and then the second part and so on, and about the time I was at the University of Virginia the last ones came out on the seven Sacraments. These are all parts of the Incarnation being celebrated ritualistically all the time.

WOFFORD: I think I hear you saying that in that grammar school debate on who's most important, Christ or Socrates, you give the day to Christ.

BUCHANAN: That's right.

Tragedy and Comedy

WOFFORD: The Socratic embodiment of Platonic ideas—that dramatic story, the life and death of Socrates—has been said to be an intimation of Christ and maybe to have influenced the later dramatists who wrote the account of Christ.

BUCHANAN: Right. That brings up another period in my religious trouble. I read the Greek tragedies in college and we did an awful lot of discussion on this. This was free reading, not merely grammar. The whole notion of tragedy became a central point of philosophical interest for me. That is, what is the essence of a tragedy? I've tried over and over again to state this in writing, in classes where I've been teaching, and I find it endlessly interesting and deeply mysterious. That is what a real tragedy is. And of course I would connect this with Socrates in the *Apology* and *Crito*. I remember once at Oxford going to a Jesuit who was having great influence at that time and laying my theory of tragedy before him and saying, "Isn't this one of the ways to see what the Incarnation is all about? And particularly the Eucharist?"

WOFFORD: I hope you can give me that theory because I thought the line of tragic heroes stops with Christ. How can you contain Christ within the concept of tragedy?

BUCHANAN: That's the answer I got very quickly from this Jesuit. That is, no matter how deeply you go into the idea of tragedy you won't find the Christian thing there. I'm still doubting that a bit for if you read an ordinary Catholic book now on the Eucharist the dramatic structure of the Mass is emphasized almost wholly, and it's a tragic story. The Mass is continually repeating a tragic drama—but it has more significance.

WOFFORD: Tragic in what sense? Pain and "Let this cup pass from me"?

BUCHANAN: Yes, but the calamity is not the essence of tragedy. The Crucifixion would be the calamity part of it, but really the idea—and here it's more than one idea—the ideas that Jesus was preaching and living and spreading to his followers had a great rise. It started with very simple beginnings, as it does in the Gospels. The story is a complication of a tragic theme. You start with an act and an idea, the plot complicates this until you reach a point in which an idea contradicts itself, and there is a great fall. Take Oedipus Tyrannus, he's the great model for this. Everything becomes self-contradictory and cosmic things happen. In Greek tragedy

17

you have the calamity and recognition coming in at the end that makes this all clear. This is the great climax in the Gospels. The Crucifixion of God, if you want to put it that way, is the highest you can run that, I suppose. But it's imitated all over. Thucydides and Herodotus both tell Greek history in tragic form. Athens is the hero in the *Peloponnesian Wars* and goes through exactly this kind of rise and fall. With Herodotus every episode becomes a little tragedy. You sometimes get comic versions in Herodotus but almost all his little stories that go to build up to the big ones are little tragedies.

WOFFORD: What is your theory of comedy?

BUCHANAN: This is an endlessly fascinating puzzle, too. Comedy follows the same pattern; as a matter of fact it's kind of an imitation of tragedy, but it's inverted. That is, the comic hero is an impostor. He follows his illusion, his impostership, to a fall, too. The purpose of the fall in a tragedy is somehow discovering something in a great revelation at the end. A comedy leads to a point where all your illusions are smashed, so it's an inverted tragedy. The boastful fellow, the buffoon, the soldier, the cook, the doctor, the favorite comic characters—are all somehow the victims. As the proposers of illusion, all these imposters get smashed.

WOFFORD: This would be the old orthodox Jewish view of Christ, wouldn't it?

BUCHANAN: I suppose it would, and a good many people now would think this, too.

WOFFORD: Most educators think this of Socrates.

BUCHANAN: Yes, very much of Socrates. People have difficulty believing that Socrates was sincere when he said, "I don't know." This could be an impostership. The last lecture I gave at St. John's at Santa Fe was how to read a Socratic dialogue as a comedy—seeing Socrates as the buffoon who punctures all the illusions around him, including his own. This is a clarifying thing. It begins dialectic, of course, in a funny way. People have connected this with the exorcism of devils. There were things you did to people possessed with devils—things to do which destroy or drive away the demons. That's what a comic character is doing. The main notion of tragedy is the purgation of pity and terror, as Aristotle puts it. But purgation also has an intellectual meaning—the clarifying of something, the revelation of something at the end. The great term is recognition. The tragic hero may be destroyed, but as he is destroyed he finds out who he is.

WOFFORD: The relation of comedy and tragedy?

BUCHANAN: Mark Van Doren and I have a continuing conversation about this. These are two views of life, not just literary or religious forms. They are two profound and ultimate views of life. And their relations to each other are very puzzling. Comedy is just as important and fundamental as tragedy.

WOFFORD: Do you alternate in which view you hold of your own life?

BUCHANAN: The sad thing about it is that you can't— I'm not making this too personal, I hope—but the individual can't quite become the tragic hero in his own eyes. He never sees this. He's blind in that way. This is one of the puzzles about tragedy. That is, you could take this doctrine, tragedy and comedy, as a kind of ethics: you should live to be a tragic hero. But you can't do this deliberately. Someone else may see it but you can't see it.

WOFFORD: Or, when you do it deliberately you become a comic figure.

BUCHANAN: Yes. You laugh at yourself at the wrong point. You see through the illusion; even when you're a fanatic you see this, and this is very disturbing. It's a problem of your own honesty. You pray for a sense of humor so you won't become a tragic hero, and then after all it isn't as comic as that. I'm not stating this very well, but for years now, probably most of my life, these have been the guiding patterns for any other thing that I've been trying to do. They are the way I understand history now; the way I understand most of the problems we're having at the Center, and all big political problems.

WOFFORD: How do you mean that?

BUCHANAN: A political career on the part of an individual or nation or institution is tragic, fundamentally, and comic if you can make it that. Thucydides is a great pattern for this. His Athens started out to be a city-state. It found itself surrounded by other city-states and, because Athens was stronger, the other ones became subordinate to it. Some of this was deliberate on the part of Athens and some of it was forced on it. There came a time when it had to fight. Sparta developed connections with other city-states and drew up lines of battle. Then, there's always a moment in a tragedy when you have the hybritic act; when the hero finds that he has no choice but to do the thing that will save his integrity. This is Athens going to Syracuse. It was a silly thing to do, an imprudent thing to do, a vile thing to do. Alcibiades precipitated it, but there wasn't anything else for him to do. He was right, fundamentally. But this was Athen's great, complete defeat. It recovered some but never completely. This happens in history. I understand Thucydides is being read in Washington now with great interest, and they're putting Vietnam in the middle of it. At St. John's all through the Second World War we were reading Thucydides over and over again with freshmen.

WOFFORD: During the early days of the Cold War, General Marshall said whenever he wanted to get light on where to go he turned to Thucydides. Then I concluded that he really meant that Athens was his side.

BUCHANAN: You have to do this. Marshall must have known this was the ruin of Athens, but you follow the Athenian thing because it's so highly rational. The intelligence of that whole people was put into this, and it was very high intelligence, a very civilized community, but caught in this awful business.

WOFFORD: Could you sketch the American tragedy as you see it? Once you said there was a moment in American history when politics was transfigured, at the time of the Constitution and the first years.

BUCHANAN: I suppose our Civil War was a great tragedy. We're now in a post-tragic state. Many tragedies can happen in serial. The Greeks gave them in trilogies. We may be on another rise now, after the Civil War. We are becoming imperial, taking on world responsibilities, and in some way most of the world is taking this for granted. They may be against it in the ordinary international politics but on the whole they are expecting us to take our responsibility. Vietnam may be our Syracuse. Maybe we're leading up to a great fall and a great recognition. This would be a great thing for us but it might be pretty calamitous.

WOFFORD: David Riesman says the thing he fears most is that we might win in Vietnam. Escalation might succeed and then we wouldn't really learn where we are.

BUCHANAN: I agree with him. The failure to be tragic is the saddest thing in life. If we don't lead to a crisis now, we may go on indefinitely with a kind of sick business, like the Greeks did. They just went on and on with episode after episode of a melodramatic character having no great significance at all.

WOFFORD: That's what politics generally is.

BUCHANAN: Yes, this is the great strain in all politics. The curious thing about the Greeks (I suppose I'm more Greek than anything else) is in some way they always

21

learned through tragedy. They may have failed in the beginning and the middle of the process, but they never failed in the end to see what had happened.

WOFFORD: You turned a circle in this, too, if I recall right. You were deeply concerned about the world and about politics during World War I. The account I have is that for many years afterward you didn't even vote. You weren't interested in politics, and it was not a central part of the curriculum you recommended. In the last fifteen or twenty years you've gone back to politics.

BUCHANAN: This is true, and puzzling. A little episode may help explain it. I was a great admirer, almost a worshipper, of Woodrow Wilson. From the very beginning of the war, right through to his death, he was for me a real tragic hero. He had the stuff that would make that happen, not only to himself but to the rest of the world.

After he died, the Woodrow Wilson Foundation was set up and they offered a prize of $25,000 for an essay on Wilson. I wanted the money to go to medical school, so, for very low reasons, I wrote an essay, and thousands of people wrote essays. My title was, "Woodrow Wilson, the Tragic Hero." In a curious way this finished my interest in politics at the time. Woodrow Wilson's death, our failure to get into the League of Nations, the relative state of politics, if you remember, after the First World War, Harding, Coolidge and Hoover and all this kind of thing, just seemed to me awful. I just had no heart for it at all. I'd never had any real training in it anyway, so I dropped the whole thing. And also I had a theory then, since the McCarthy period I've wondered how I thought this, but at that time I had a theory that a teacher shouldn't be involved in politics.

WOFFORD: Why?

BUCHANAN: I was taking academic freedom and the functions of a teacher very seriously and saying any effect you have on politics should be indirect. You should teach others the best you can and hope they're political, but you shouldn't be political yourself. You should be intellectual, academic—and this is the reason you protect academic freedom. A teacher should be protected from politics both ways. He shouldn't be influenced by it and shouldn't take part in it either. So it was a kind of conversion at the end of the Second World War when I went in for politics so strongly. After I left St. John's, I went back the next year—I was asked to give a lecture—and argued that the whole program ought to be about law and politics. Then I tried to do something about it myself, with some crazy results. I can't explain in detail. If I were the kind to put my life together, this would be one of the themes I'd have to do something about. I'd have to dig up a lot of stuff I don't remember.

Following the Question

WOFFORD: Was the idea of following the question where it leads an early, deliberate, dominant thing—a conscious way of proceeding through your education?

BUCHANAN: I don't know when that started but probably while doing the dialogues with the adult students in New York it came out. At Amherst, under Meiklejohn, lecturing was a kind of sin. He talked about Socratic methods and used them in everything he could, as did I, even when I was teaching Greek. I have done it in all the discussion groups we have had. So I never learned to lecture. I haven't any art when I lecture.

I'm not any good at it because I took the Socratic doctrine seriously. You follow the argument, discussion, dialectic. It was the only way people learned. This is because discussions are kind of tragic, too.

WOFFORD: We are trying to take a radical turn in Peace Corps training from lectures to seminars. The reports coming back, on balance, support the turn but they also include dire accounts of unhappy and unsuccessful discussions, and bad discussion leaders, and not just because some of the former lecturers thought a discussion meant sitting around a table and lecturing. Some of the unhappiest occasions were when they were really trying to have a discussion and nobody said very much.

BUCHANAN: The whole academic community shifts like a big iceberg from one thing to another, almost inexorably. Discussion is not understood any more as it was then at Amherst. You have discussion classes, yes, but it's understood as a curious way of vicarious lecturing, that is, get students to lecture instead of you, and you lead them heavily in this kind of thing.

WOFFORD: In some places the students are now rebelling and rising with the claim, "We'll teach ourselves." They're determined to break this line between student and teacher. When you were talking about the good · teachers at Amherst, how did they handle this?

BUCHANAN: The people that Alec got to come, all of these people were leaders of discussion—all of them. They could lecture but, as I said, it became a sin. The old faculty was lecturing and this became sort of a campus civil war between the two schools of thought. But the discussion idea spread, and some of the old teachers learned to do it. It was a funny illusion, but when I got out of Amherst I was shocked and surprised to find lecturing was still going on in other places. Yet there was a period in the twenties when a lot of people were teaching by discussion. There are reasons why it shifted—one, of course, is it is not easy to do this when you are teaching natural sciences.

WOFFORD: Too many facts.

BUCHANAN: Yes, a laboratory takes over with lots of other techniques, and you want to get across as much as you can. The mechanical teaching now being done has a lot of this in it. That is, the student is in some peculiar discussional relation with the teaching machine. He answers a question, the machine says No. It is a pretty low kind of discussion but there's some in it.

WOFFORD: The theory of learning by immediate feedback has application to a seminar. In programmed instruction, you know you're right immediately; often in a seminar you suddenly see something and it may be even generally recognized around the table.

BUCHANAN: Yes, but this is individual. You can't be sure everyone has got it. Yet this is *the* thing you're after in a good discussion: individual insight. You're not after agreement or a doctrine or anything of this sort.

WOFFORD: Some Socratic dialogues, at least if read badly, seem to be the other kind of teaching in which Socrates is directing the others to the answers he knows and to the destination he has decided on in advance.

BUCHANAN: This is a puzzle. The early dialogues are very Socratic in the sense he's always asking questions without knowing the answers—the *Crito,* the *Apology,* the *Ion,* the *Protagoras,* the *Gorgias.* The *Symposium* shifts a bit. These are lectures in a funny way, although Socrates finally turned his talk into a discussion. In the *Republic* it's hard to believe Socrates is playing his old stuff, and yet you get the feel of it. Socrates is talking at length on certain things, but the effect on his hearers is a question. Even there, if you read it well, you realize there is no doctrine in *The Republic*. Socrates is proposing something and saying, "Now, what about this? Dare I go on with this sort of thing?" The later post-*Republic* dialogues are very puzzling because Socrates disappears in most of them. Someone else plays another kind of role. The person who seems to take the place of Socrates is called the Stranger and he's longwinded. The yarns are endless. There's almost no real discussion. Yet in Plato's letters, especially the Seventh and the Thirteenth, he's so strong on the written word not being the way you convey anything, on a lecture not being the way, you almost get to the point where you think speech is not the way. What he is emphasizing is this insight that happens in the middle of the discussion. That is what is understanding; the other stuff is lumber.

Even the doctrine of ideas is not really a Platonic doctrine. It came from the Pythagorans. Everyone was entertaining this in Athens. Plato finally criticizes it so it doesn't stand up any more. These are all questions he has been raising. A question can be very elaborate and can be a long discourse. When you get to be my age, you read every book as a question. You're not reading for information nor for doctrine or anything else. You want to entertain this idea, you want to explore that one.

We were just discussing some papers done at the Center here on "The Civilization of the Dialogue." It was an attempt to see a whole society as involved in a Socratic dialogue. Spontaneously—not as though someone goes out and tries to organize discussion groups. Dialogue is what politics means, what everything in our society means—a vast dialogue going on all the time, with discoveries made of the Socratic kind. Leaders, whether they're Socratic or not, whether they behave that way, have this final effect: they are in effect questioning the society they live in and bringing out answers. Of course, this has been made fashionable now by Kierkegaard and Buber, who make dialogue the dominant theme. And as the church renovates itself, as it has during the Vatican Council meetings, it comes back wanting to be in dialogical relation with the world. Very few teachers in universities are doing this, but the great institutions of our society are, and understanding themselves that way.

WOFFORD: When did you start seeing that you may not know much, but that most of the teachers you met knew less? You must go through that process because I've seen you puncturing many an imposter.

BUCHANAN: This started at Amherst. I know I used to be a little afraid of it at first. I thought, "I'm a dangerous fellow, going around making a quarrel with everyone I meet, even people who know a lot more than I do. What's this all about?" I suppose Plato interested me more at that point than he ever had before. What was Socrates really doing? Was he the gadfly and nasty fellow he seems to be, and is this a good thing to be? I ran across this again in a very vivid way when I was teaching at Fisk in the 1950's. I had a class of rather superior students. I hadn't asked them to be chosen this way but they wanted me to have a special class of some of the best seniors. We read all the Plato we could. Right away the students, I felt, feared and hated Socrates, and then it got worse. They couldn't take him straight. About the middle of the year three came to see me one afternoon and we spent hours talking. I was saying what I thought the university was about and what Socratic teaching was doing, and finally the best student there said, "Do you realize what would happen to us if we took Socrates seriously?" He went on with some suggestions of what it would be for a Negro to be a Socratic character in our society. All the stuff that has gone on since then for civil rights has in some way been Socratic. But at that point, in 1956, they saw it coming and were scared to their toes. They tried to make me see that I was asking them, teasing them, tempting them to their destruction. They had understood better than I had, I think, what Socrates was.

WOFFORD: I remember in 1950 Antonio Borgese called you the great destroyer. Do you still have the courage and presumption to prescribe Socrates to Negroes, to Peace Corps volunteers, to all Americans?

BUCHANAN: Yes, though now I can't claim courage; it's habit. I don't know anything else to do.

WOFFORD: I get accused occasionally of endangering and damaging the lives of people who get led into more unsettlement and turbulence than they can handle.

BUCHANAN: What do you do? You can't stop, can you, once you see the point that the central thing is to get some understanding—I wish there were a better word—some insight, something beside just rigamarole and rhetoric? Even direct action calls for this—it is the real point of street demonstrations and sit-ins. Gandhi gives a deeper interpretation: all of action, not merely speech and thought, has this dialogical character. You've been up against this more than I have.

WOFFORD: I've been trying to use seminars as a way of learning in the midst of all kinds of actions, but, as you say, a seminar can have a tragic course, and the saddest course is when it doesn't become tragic but just fizzles. Our problem with seminars in Peace Corps training may be that the trainees haven't been over there yet. Some of the returned volunteers say, "We're ready to read Plato now. Liberal education is not that we've had in college or in the Peace Corps, but what we're ready for." I wonder whether you need some grist of experience to go into the Platonic mill. That's why I'm pressing you on whether the experience of World War I was part of the reason this thing came alive for you.

At the University of Chicago, after World War II, the discussion was the most vivid thing in my life, but in retrospect it wasn't just because the books we read are great, or that we sat around the table and followed the questions fairly well. Perhaps it worked in part because two-thirds of the people sitting around the table were veterans, who had faced danger or frustration somewhere in the war.

BUCHANAN: Then, too, your acquaintance with the whole Gandhian thing in India did that for you, too, later.

WOFFORD: It sounds so Dewey-ite, you know, learning by doing, but that isn't quite what I'm saying.

BUCHANAN: No. The history of the idea of the dialectic in our whole western tradition throws some light on this. I suppose the Greeks, through Socrates, did discover the dialectic in some very subtle and high form. This is about as high as human discourse has ever gone.

WOFFORD: And it came out of a lot of action. These were dialogues with people who were in the world, who were citizens, many of them had been engaged or were about to be engaged in great actions. Socrates was talking with people—and soared high with people—who were going out to wage war, to make love, even to commit treason.

BUCHANAN: Yes, in some ways the most interesting of the dialogues were the two with generals, Laches and Meno, who didn't understand what Socrates was saying, but he was drawing them out about courage and learning in an eloquent way. You can say the Greeks were developing out of human experience of the kind you are speaking of and were developing the verbal, literary and philosophical disciplines to go with this. Then it jumps to the Middle Ages and you find people doing this with religion. The great disputations of the Middle Ages were, in a sense, dealing with a heavy human experience again. It sounds to us like logic chopping and spinning of doctrines but for them religion was a heavy burden of human experience they had to clarify in some way. And then you get the modern dialectic from Hegel and Marx, doing more of what you were just talking about. That is, the verbal dialectic is enmeshed in and is harnessed to the great movements in history.

The modern dialectic is not to refine this into some elaborate play, but almost the reverse, to see that the rationality you discover in the word, in the talk, moves in history in some way. The Cold War and the clash of ideologies, if you like, is a great dialectic going on between two systems of ideas, but it goes deeper. These are heavy economic, political, moral, passionate issues. The dialectic is a great tool, not only of history, but of practical politics at the same time, and of religion. The religious dialectic that's going on now is the most amazing, surprising thing. It could be a great renaissance happening in the world of intellectual things, and it could be a failure, it could go flat, because in some sense we are not, in this country at present, dialectical in spirit at all.

WOFFORD: This is a hard time for good seminars.

BUCHANAN: It certainly is. The seminar table may be a victim of all this. You are almost surprised if you can do a good job talking now, because the weight is so heavy that you're dealing with.

WOFFORD: You do believe that everybody is a Silenus? Alcibiades hurls this charge at Socrates.

BUCHANAN: Yes. It was his description of Socrates—an ugly statue which you open up and find beautiful images of the gods inside.

WOFFORD: Who is Silenus?

BUCHANAN: A little god, not very important, I think; a trinket they had around, like the things kids have now that open up and you find something surprising inside. But this happened to have a beautiful little image inside. Alcibiades was making fun of Socrates, saying this was Socrates' character; but he touched the great insight of Socrates that every human being is of this kind. If you examine him, if he examines himself with the help of a dialectician, you and he will discover that he is like that, and if you go on, you will find that all men are like that: they have minds, can think, ask questions and answer them, discover who they are, what the world's about and a whole lot of things.

WOFFORD: And they have something in them that would surprise you?

BUCHANAN: Yes, they're always surprising.

WOFFORD: They still surprise you?

BUCHANAN: This is a common experience to me. You have setbacks. You have the comic version. You can look at somebody and begin to treat him as important and able and all this kind of thing, and you ask him a few questions and he falls to pieces. There's a good deal of that around at present, but that's only an incitement to carry on with the business. Dialectic can even be, as it is now being used in psychiatry, a way of recovery from having fallen to pieces. Group therapy is another kind of practice of this. We're not really very close to Plato or Socrates but "know thyself" can be applied on all levels. You can be superficial or you can be deep.

WOFFORD: I take it a deep psychoanalysis, too, can be endangering?

BUCHANAN: Yes. Its aim, of course, is to bring about some actual integration but it tends to pull people to pieces and if it isn't carried through to real insight it can be very very demoralizing and destructive, extremely so. Following the argument wherever it leads may mean a very, very long route. It isn't a quick way to recover. It can be, but often it is a very distant thing. You know, even Socrates said—or Plato makes him say—that dialectic is a dangerous thing for young men. In the education proposed in *The Republic* you don't go into dialectic in the first stages at all; only from the age of thirty-five to fifty. I don't hold this as an educational principle but it does say something about the conditions for dialectic really working in this high form.

Poetry and Mathematics

WOFFORD: Your education over 70 years is a hopeful thing since it seems to continue. I'm interested in how it began and what the main elements and factors were.
BUCHANAN: I might begin with my first school in the village in Vermont where we lived at the turn of the century. Jeffersonville was a small town, probably not over a thousand inhabitants. There was a schoolhouse in the middle of the town next door to our house, so I was watching the children even before I went to school. It was a curious school with four rooms that included everything from the first grade through high school. There were three grades in each room and recitations were held in front of the room in rotation. From the very start I was listening to classes ahead of me and then, as I went on, to classes behind me. So I had a sort of a triple education. I had to prepare my own work but I was also watching the teaching and learning a good deal from the other classes as I went on. It made me realize very early how much teaching goes on between students. Pupils were arranged by class standing. There was the first one, the second, the third or whatever the number was—ten or fifteen—and you shifted your position according to whether you did well or not.

You got your marks, so to speak, every day. If you did something well, you moved up. What this meant was there was a hierarchy and the learning process was going back and forth.

WOFFORD: That didn't corrupt the community of learning? The demand of students today in higher education is to get rid of grading and marks.

BUCHANAN: These weren't grades but a substitute for them—a more direct and immediate kind of thing. The competition involved was not the main point. There was a certain kind of leadership and followership, and at some point I discovered the slower students often were teaching the better students as much as the other direction.

WOFFORD: How?

BUCHANAN: They were holding them up to the things the fast ones were skipping over. You'd hear something all over again and know that you'd missed it. Since then I've always seen a classroom as a very lively relationship between mutual teachers. In our present crisis in education with large classes and shortage of teachers, we have either blotted out this process or have ignored it. I suspect the latter. If we paid more attention to the kind of learning going on between pupils, we would realize what they now call the "multiplier effect" of any teaching. The teacher just starts it and it goes on from one person to another throughout the class. This may be a phenomenon of the small district school, but I've never forgotten it and I'll never forget the kind of ecstasy I had on occasion when I was learning something from what was going on on the other side of the room.

WOFFORD: Did you often have that ecstasy when you were learning from people in the back of the room? Learning from people who were ahead of you I can more easily imagine than learning from those who were behind you.

BUCHANAN: Sometimes there was something that I'd missed and something very important would come out. This must mean we had some pretty good teachers because they were paying attention to the slow ones and things were being integrated in some curious way. I may exaggerate this but I remember it as being a great pleasure on occasion. Not always, it was sometimes a bore, of course, and once in a while we had a bad teacher. I remember a man teacher with very red hair and a quick, bad temper. One time I gave what seemed to him a very flippant answer. He thought I was being fresh. I was more or less suspended from class and had to go for one term to school three miles away in another village. For some reason this heightened my attention to the whole business. I remember two or three things I learned in that strange school where I wasn't very well known. For the first time I understood rhetoric. We were reading a textbook on rhetoric as an assignment and I began understanding figures of speech, and I never cease being interested in this whole subject. This was exciting and got me going. It belongs, as I learned later, to the trivium, a very important part of it.

WOFFORD: What is the trivium?

BUCHANAN: Grammar, rhetoric and logic. Rhetoric, at least a great part of the subject matter, is figures of speech—metaphors, analogies, allegories, metonymy, synecdoche, and all these things. Sometimes they are a matter of idiom, sometimes a matter of invention in poetry, but they are useful in most extraordinary ways when you watch them. Rhetoric is not merely making speeches. I've been recently trying to write about law, and I find when I look over the things I've read in law, particularly on the judicial process, almost all the reasoning is by analogy. The whole system of case precedents starts with an initial sort of archetypal case, and the cases are lined up after this. The law grows through analogy. You never get an abstraction out of this. Lawyers don't like to. Of course it has something to do with the very difficult intellectual process that goes on in a courtroom—making a general law apply to a specific case with all its special circumstances and details. The law is general and as you start the reasoning, you're not sure it's going to apply, but you make it apply through a series of analogies, or precedents.

This same thing came up when I was doing philosophy of medicine. This is the way diagnosis works, too. You identify disease through a syndrome of patterns, analogous with each other.

So analogy is a very powerful instrument of learning. You turn this into mathematics and it becomes the whole theory of ratios and proportions that leads into the basic modern mathematics. It's in algebra. It is a very important thing to know about, it seems to me, and to consciously cultivate if you can. And I think the reason I got interested in this is because of that little fracas I had when I went to another school. I can see that rhetoric textbook now, a very exciting book. It wasn't one of these modern jazzed-up textbooks; it was old-fashioned, but everything in it was telling me what I wanted to know.

WOFFORD: You are saying there are some fundamental processes of thinking one can use to learn anything.

BUCHANAN: Yes, of course. This is what the trivium is all about. The Greeks identified these sciences and arts. Grammar, rhetoric, and logic are the ways the human mind deals with the world. The only way it knows how is by words and figures of speech and inflections, and if you don't know this you can be puzzled and deceived. You can deceive yourself and get into some of the curious corners we are in now. Almost all of our modern science is grammatical. The words apply to things and that's all, not to abstractions. But our science need not be empirical; it could be abstract if we thought about it in another way. People say, "Oh, abstraction is dangerous; you mustn't go into that," and the same way with figures of speech. Almost everybody says analogy is a dangerous way of reasoning. But it's a fundamental way of reasoning in the great professions, and for all of us, as a matter of fact.

WOFFORD: Do you teach these methods separately, in a subject like rhetoric, or do you teach it by teaching law, for example?

BUCHANAN: I should think it should be done in connection with language study or some other subject matter; law would be a very good one for analogies. Almost anything will carry the analogies. But there is a problem about liberal education: if you want to return to anything like a liberal college at present, what subject matter would do it best for this? As you and I have said for a long time law would be good for this, and now you are saying theology and medicine, too, and I follow you. We have to get the great subject matters into the curriculum in order to draw out the greatest power of the arts and the sciences that are called liberal. At St. John's we were using great books for this. We were saying the great books are the great masterpieces of the liberal arts. You can also say the professions are constructions or occupations or disciplines which apply the liberal arts. If you want to learn the liberal arts you'd better have great subject matter that will stretch them to their full capacities.

WOFFORD: How much can be done before college?

BUCHANAN: A great deal. If our secondary schools were doing their job well almost all of the fundamental things could be done there. They are in Europe in the gymnasium and the lycee. They are faithful to the old view of language and mathematics being the medium in which you have to be master in order to do any kind of thinking. At some point there has to be discipline—and that doesn't mean discipline in the punishment sense; it means learning. People forget the word discipline means learning—acquiring habits. These have to be acquired. These have to be second nature or they don't work.

WOFFORD: Where do you put poetry? I once recall your prescribing heavy doses of poetry for early adolescence. We were imagining once a new kind of primary and secondary school.

BUCHANAN: This question was always put to us at St. John's: what would you do if you were teaching in a primary school? The answer we cooked up was there would be a great deal of poetry, to get the imagination wakened and moving easily. That's necessary to do the liberal arts. Imagination is the medium in which all these are done, and poetry is a powerful force. It is hard to say just why, but poetry is, as you know, the oldest of the written—even of the spoken—disciplines. Even before there was writing, there was poetry. In fact poetry probably existed before there was anything like prose. It was passed on by word of mouth That's the reason why rhymes and metrics and all that sort of thing come into it. It is a good memory medium and of course memory is closely related to imagination. In fact the ancients call everything we call imagination just memory. So poetry is the medium, and I don't know why it stops. I have a suspicion now adult education ought to be chiefly in the medium of poetic forms—highly developed ones, dramas, and great long poems like *The Iliad* or the *Divine Comedy* or Shakespeare.

WOFFORD: I think poetry may have been the central factor that keeps me awakened, and one of the first factors that woke me at all.

BUCHANAN: Do you remember what hit you? Jingles, when you were a small child?

WOFFORD: I don't remember that. American poetry. I had a heavy romance with America when I was twelve or thirteen and it isn't over yet.

BUCHANAN: Do you memorize poetry easily?

WOFFORD: No.

BUCHANAN: This is another thing that puzzles me. When I was a child and first went to school, I could memorize almost anything. I can't any more—I have almost no rote memory left. You have it in your ordinary speech, of course, a lot of it, but I can't sit down and memorize a paragraph or a poem now. I always make a mistake when I try to repeat it. But I was quite good when I was young. It must have been when I was nine years old, I was put on the stage for a Patriot's Day celebration in our little town. I had memorized "Paul Revere's Ride," and it still sticks.

WOFFORD: That was on my list. And Poe and Whitman. Can you list central poems that stick with you?

BUCHANAN: Oh, a good deal of Eliot does. Hopkins. Some Yeats. Emily Dickinson. No, I can't discourse on this. This is something deep in your subconscious and comes up when you try to write, too much so with me.

WOFFORD: Did you have a lot of mathematics before you went to college?

BUCHANAN: From first grade on. I did algebra and geometry in high school and happened to have some good old-fashioned teachers for those subjects, sort of rigorous, downright people who had no nonsense about them. They were very wise and skillful at teaching. Mathematics hit me hard because of a teacher I had at Amherst, Charles Cobb, a very unconventional teacher. His mathematics classes were all seminar. We were always trying to find out not just how you did the problems—in fact he was rather weak on that and got criticized by his colleagues for it a great deal—but what these structures really meant. When we were doing calculus his favorite question would be: "What is a function?" The whole idea of functions in mathematics changes as you do calculus. He must have asked this on an average of once a month, and you'd give it a different answer every time because you were learning more about it. So mathematics became a very lively subject for me, a wonderful sort of inventive thing. I'm not very good at doing sums, or solving algebraic equations, or integrating a function, but I find mathematics is a whole world I can move around in—up to a point where I don't understand it any more. Very late, at Harvard, I did a great deal of mathematical logic and that awakened a lot of algebra for me, algebraic modes of thinking anyway, and what the possibilities were in that sort of thing. Then there was a great excitement ten years later when I was teaching philosophy at the University of Virginia. I went to the classes of a friend who was teaching geometry and learned the other kinds of geometry besides the Euclidian. The really modern stuff I'm not up on at all and can't understand a lot of, but I can now read a mathematics book with the same kind of interest that I read a verbal article. Not many people have had this advantage, but this is what Charlie Cobb taught us to do. He never taught us to do *that* but I found I could do it—with considerable interest. I mean it's exciting. And if you do it you tend to do a great deal of other thinking in mathematical modes. This used to worry me a good deal. I thought I was misreading a good deal of philosophical work because I was understanding it in terms of mathematical forms and, to a certain extent, this was bad because I was translating it too fast into mathematical patterns. But it is a very penetrating way. This somehow supports my Platonism, if I am a Platonist in any sense, because Plato's dialogues sometimes do discuss mathematics straight, and they are all mathematical in form: the arguments are mathematical propositions.

WOFFORD: What do you mean?

BUCHANAN: You know there are many kinds of logic but the ordinary Aristotelian logic is built on the notion of syllogisms, concepts being ordered, subsuming species in general, and so forth. Plato's thinking is all in terms of relations. There are big classifications but when Plato really gets going on something he shifts to relational logic, and relations are the basis of mathematics. You can see an analogy more sharply when it's in a mathematical proportion. One is to two as three is to six, or something like this. The analogy is saying the same thing in verbal terms. The emphasis is on the relations between the terms you're watching. When you say one is to two as three is to six you are saying the relation between one and two is the same as the relation between three and six, and that's what you want to see.

WOFFORD: If this is true, your prescription of law and mathematics as the center of a liberal arts curriculum might close Snow's two-culture gap. If non-science people learn mathematics they would cross that gap.

BUCHANAN: Law is quite mathematical without the lawyers knowing it. When lawyers say analogy they don't really analyze what an analogy is. They're artists with it, and use it rapidly and well. But if they wanted to turn around on it and say, "What's this about?", they would find the form is like mathematics. Now, of course, I have to shift my terminology a bit because if this relational stuff is mathematical then a lot of verbal stuff is mathematics, and you can play back and forth with these two things. But there's an independent tradition. The trivium and the quadrivium (the four sciences in mathematics) are parallels. Arithmetic and geometry are the grammar of mathematics; the rhetoric or analogies of mathematics would be the ratios and proportions; and the logic of mathematics would be function.

Mathematics tends to take an abstraction and make it point to particulars. It makes you look for facts as you do in physics, you see. Whereas verbal analogies tend to make you look toward abstractions. They climb, whereas mathematics tends to go down. Actually to do a good job in either one you have to cross over, back and forth, but most people don't know they're doing that; they do it automatically. That is the reason why I have a very deep conviction, or what I like to call insight, that mathematics and language are indigenous to the human soul. You cannot move in thought without using these complicated and echoing ways with each other. This is what I think I discovered for myself in *Poetry and Mathematics.*

WOFFORD: Are you talking about your book?

BUCHANAN: Yes. Perhaps I ought to say how that was written. I was Assistant Director of the People's Institute in New York. I had charge of all the lectures and acted as chairman for the big lectures twice a week in the Great Hall at Cooper Union. We always had questions at the end so there was some discussion, sometimes very long discussion, and I had to interpret the questions partly because of the acoustics. This made me pay attention to what the troubles in the audience were. After two or three years of this, I generalized to this extent: it seemed to me the ordinary adult audience was missing in poetic understanding and missing in mathematical understanding. I tried to get separate lecturers to lecture on poetry and on mathematics but I couldn't get anybody to do this well enough. Finally I undertook to give these lectures myself. When I began, I realized there were these curious corresponding patterns in poetry and mathematics that reflected each other. This is where I discovered, without knowing it, the trivium and the quadrivium. It was Dick McKeon who told me at the end that this was what I had been doing. Then Mortimer

Adler, Dick McKeon and I went after the liberal arts in a very concerted way, trying to make them up-to-date.

WOFFORD: The harder case is to get people who love poetry and read literature and go into politics to understand why they need mathematics to understand the other world we're living in. I think this is harder than getting men of science and mathematics to seek poetry or read literature or participate in politics.

BUCHANAN: I'm not sure one is more difficult than the other. C. P. Snow is right about the two cultures, up to this point anyway. There is a great split now, and it's hard to persuade either one to think it has any responsibility for the other.

WOFFORD: Was this so at Amherst in 1916?

BUCHANAN: Sure. It's been so right along. The history of the liberal arts is a history of battles between the two cultures. C. P. Snow didn't discover anything new. There have been very few times when there's been an even development of the two. In fact, it almost looks as if, at any given time, if you cultivate one side of this, you can't do the other. The simultaneous development of these seems impossible. But in the best times, with the Greeks and in the Middle Ages and the Renaissance, there were some great minds at least—and of course other people imitating or following—who had this balance. It's extraordinary when you see it. Plato, of course, is the great case. But take Thomas Aquinas: he's not a mathematician, in fact he was quite restricted in that, but the forms of thought he uses are mathematical. The great bridge that we have at present is our constant use of measurement. That's the application of numbers to verbal and concrete things, back and forth, all the time. You have to verbalize the concrete things in order to know what you're measuring, and measurement is our greatest business at present—in everything. And the tricks in measurements, the inventions in it, are tremendous with all the instruments that go with it. The laboratories know all about this.

WOFFORD: Where does medicine come into this? You said for a while you wanted to become a doctor.

BUCHANAN: This goes back to my father. He was a physician, before the turn of the century, a country doctor. He died when I was seven years old but he had some wish I should be a doctor. The last words he ever said to me were to ask me if I was going to be a doctor. And this I've never forgotten, of course. But it can't be just those words that did it to me. I was interested in medicine very much. He was apparently a good doctor in the old fashioned sense. I felt this, because before he died I often used to go on visits to patients with him, and I felt the function of medicine and the person very much. So for a long time—all through high school until I got to Amherst—education was leading me towards medical school. Then a funny thing happened to me, one of those educational accidents, or a youthful misjudgment, I suppose. I took chemistry in my freshman year, and I got a hundred in it, but I realized I hadn't understood anything, I'd just done my lessons well—just rigamarole, but I'd done it perfectly. And the next year I took biology and got very much interested and did a good job in it—and almost flunked it, got a "D." I said to myself, "This kind of confusion means I'm not a scientist. I'm misunderstanding everything I'm doing. I thought I did well in biology and terribly in chemistry, but the judgment of my betters is the other way." This shook me badly and I didn't go on with science very much. I should have. I would have been interested to go on in physics and all the other things.

WOFFORD: Did you major?

BUCHANAN: Yes, but I majored in a funny way. I didn't concentrate. I had three majors when I got through, instead of one, and a scattering of other studies. I had majored in mathematics and Greek and French—three years in each.

WOFFORD: If you had to do it again would you put that much emphasis on foreign languages?

BUCHANAN: This is another accident that led me into the trivium and quadrivium. These were the courses I got at Amherst in a wide-open elective system. By accidents of scheduling (I had to work my way through, so I couldn't take some classes because I was waiting on table at that time) I came out with these things. I took some economics and I took some—what are all those things?—English literature, a good deal of that, a little history, not much of anything else.

WOFFORD: What did you think you were going to do when you left Amherst?

BUCHANAN: I wasn't sure but I had gotten deeply interested in philosophy. In a sense, I had majored in that, too, but not technically. We had rather bad teachers of philosophy then. Alec Meiklejohn was around. I never took a course with him but I learned a lot of philosophy just by knowing him.

Meiklejohn, Lincoln and the Republic

WOFFORD: Then Meiklejohn, for you, was Socrates?

BUCHANAN: Yes, I suppose that connected me with Plato at this point. I did Kant with a little group in Alec's study—about five members of the faculty, and I was included.

WOFFORD: Not a credit course?

BUCHANAN: Oh, no, no credits at all. This was just as good. There were some very interesting people— economists, psychologists, mathematicians and so on. I don't know how they allowed me in. I knew Alec pretty well, I guess. He let me in.

WOFFORD: I want to hear why he was Socrates.

BUCHANAN: At the time I was excited by Alec but it took me the rest of his life to understand and appreciate what went on during the eleven years he was there. He came from Brown, and announced in his inaugural speech that the American college was in disarray and needed overhauling. This was an eloquent and great announcement. But there was no great reform initiated right away. Alec was doing things with the faculty and with students a good deal, and he began a curious kind of questioning of everything—Why are we doing this? Why are we doing that? Sometimes these led into quite lengthy dialogues. I hadn't read much Plato then, but as I recognized later, this was a very Socratic administration. He wasn't just doing this for conversational purposes; it was his way of beginning to get inside the college and see what to do about it. Slowly he brought in new members of the faculty who had something of this quality about them. They were all looking at the educational process, the curriculum, the organization of the college, and saying, "Why do we do that? Why do we do this?"

This was very catching. Students began doing it too. For a few years, while I was an undergraduate and for another four years after that—I was around for two of those—Amherst was a very dialectical college. Fraternity houses were full of this kind of thing. Just ordinary conversations took on a new quality and we were going after each other intellectually—asking questions and driving people into corners and sometimes coming out with rather remarkable results. Sometimes it was just bad feeling, because this kind of thing, as you can guess, would set up a certain kind of hostility, the same kind Socrates got in Athens. People didn't like it. But there were other people that took to it, like young men do, and made fools of themselves. They went after it very hard.

WOFFORD: Hard enough to be dangerous to the institution or the young men—to really stir them up to fundamental changes in their lives?

BUCHANAN: That was certainly true of the people that followed Alec, and even with the people that were in opposition—they got sore enough so they got disturbed. Members of my class still hate Alec Meiklejohn. When they go for a reunion, they are apt to parody his little speeches in chapel. He still is a thing to kick around.

WOFFORD: The majority of your class disliked him—were dismayed by him?

BUCHANAN: Yes. You see, he was getting some new curriculum going, but none of us had much advantage of this. I never took anything from any of his new people. I got to know them well and joined them in their informal sessions but very few of my class did this. The Class of 1918 was about the first one to be wholly Meiklejohnian. It was a great business. They began a course called Social and Economic Institutions in their freshman year, and this had started them all off on new kinds of questions and wakened them up. The rest of the curriculum wasn't always useful to them but they were looking around for things that would go with what they had started in their freshman year. Then the classes became seminars and discussions rather than lectures, not wholly, but perhaps half the college turned over this way. Those who weren't doing it were on the defensive. They thought this was barbarian stuff that they were up against and they couldn't do it. They felt it every day and they were pressed by it. Then things blew up. The hostility spread to the alumni and the trustees and, finally, after eleven years, Alec resigned.

WOFFORD: By that time, what proportion of the student body do you think was with him?

BUCHANAN: Very hard to say. Some I meet might have been for Meiklejohn when they graduated, but they're not now because they have been with the alumni and have heard all this hostility, this criticism of Alec's regime. He was charged with being a bad administrator because of this new form of administration. Recently, Rosemary Park, President of Barnard, gave a speech at the Los Angeles Conference on Universities called by our Center. Part of her paper stated the function of an administrator that fitted Alec almost perfectly. He ought to be questioning his faculty about everything they're doing, and the students too, she said. This was just what Alec was doing. Of course, this would break up the ordinary administrative procedures pretty badly. It tends to split rather than integrate a community, at least at the start, and may get almost impossible to go on. It's like Socrates in Athens. Socrates felt the same kind of antipathy and finally had to drink the hemlock. Rosemary Park should have warned anyone who was following her advice that he would probably end up that way. It could work if it were tolerated more. The trustees made a judgment that Amherst couldn't stand that much disorder—couldn't stand to learn that way.

Alec was about to do the final trick on his curriculum just as he was leaving. He was appointing a lawyer, Thomas Reed Powell, to teach a senior course in law. The course in social and economic institutions would be the beginning and this would lead through a lot of social sciences and those things, literature and everything else, but it would finally end with a course in law for undergraduates, not for lawyers. Powell didn't come when Meiklejohn was fired.

I hadn't got this whole story together until Alec was at St. John's. One day he came into my office and said, "Do you know, what you're doing here is what I was trying to do at Amherst and didn't know it." Five years later he wouldn't have said this because he got concerned about certain things at St. John's, but he said it that day with great emphasis and I got him to talk more about what he'd done at Amherst. He had come with a thoroughly conceived notion of what a democratic faculty would be, and he hoped by his Socratic administration to sting them into some kind of intellectual activities so they would become an intellectual community and would themselves build the curriculum. He injected certain new members of the faculty to do this with, people that were more lively and probably abler than the older members; but on the whole he had been a democrat. He had been trying to persuade the faculty by his Socratic administration of things that they really believed, as they discovered themselves what a curriculum ought to be.

What he meant at St. John's was that we had discovered a pattern for a real curriculum. It might not have been one the Amherst faculty would have discovered, but we had a whole pattern. Because of the way we came to St. John's, we could lay it out and invite people to join us as stated, whereas he would have had his in perhaps twenty years. If he had been there that long, he would have come out with something like it.

WOFFORD: In the last years of his life—in his 70's and 80's—Meiklejohn concentrated on the issue of political freedom. He wrote his great little book, *Free Speech,* arguing that free political speech was not so much the right of an individual as the need of the body politic, for its self-government. He came to our law firm in Washington for a seminar on this, and acted just as you described—at age 80, I think. Are you agreeing with him that, Plato to the contrary notwithstanding, there's a direct connection between the Socratic process and democracy?

BUCHANAN: Yes, basic democratic process seems to me Socratic. All the members of the community should be becoming Socrateses with each other. This is fundamental democratic process. Representation, votes, majorities and all that kind of thing we make so much of is just the machinery of democracy. What you want to have happening among citizens is a Socratic kind of persuasion, it seems to me.

WOFFORD: Can a republic ever really be a learning community in that sense? Can a community of learning really be republican?

BUCHANAN: I think so. It isn't so much, "Could we make such a thing?" as "Can we see our own life in this light?" Recently we have been having some papers written about civilization and dialogue. The trouble is people have been saying, "Now we do this here—around this table—we have a civilization of the dialogue. How do we get the rest of the community to do this?" My criticism of these papers is: Why can't we get outside the walls of this room? Our whole society is doing this, and we don't know it. In lowly ways, for society doesn't go very far on the intellectual side, but bargaining is a form of question and answer. Persuasion is going on at all levels, not merely in politics and religion. You can see the whole society this way. What you hope to do with it is to improve its quality.

WOFFORD: If you see it that way.

BUCHANAN: Once you see it that way—improve those Socratic processes.

WOFFORD: When you said that once in American history, in the founding period, our politics was transfigured, you meant it was approaching this, it was seeing itself this way, it was illuminated by this kind of idea?

BUCHANAN: I'm not sure I can pick out anyone who

was seeing it that way and would have stated it the way I'm stating it, but the behavior of the founding fathers was very much like this. I've forgotten when I made that statement but it was long long ago.

WOFFORD: It stuck.

BUCHANAN: It seems to me that from the beginning of the Constitution up to the Civil War this was going on. I'm following Bryce when I say this. He thinks this was happening. Almost all politics swung around the federal principle, and the federal principle, if you understand it a certain way, is a dialectical process, a very strong one. Federalism is not just unionism, it is also the idea that there are many different communities in this, and they're persuading each other down as far as the citizens. Bryce says the Civil War stopped this, and it had not recovered when he was writing in the late 19th century. I'm impressed with this picture. It's a kind of tragic pattern. The American republic was a real republic until the Civil War when it contradicted itself and fell to pieces for the time being, and it hasn't really recovered since in the political sense.

WOFFORD: You can see Lincoln as the most Socratic person in American history?

BUCHANAN: I think that's true. He had a lot of traits that are not Socratic in the obvious sense, but there is this: he was a brooder. This is the word used about him so much. He was listening in a curious way to what was going on throughout the community—kind of a brooding presence over the whole thing. People forget this side of Socrates. They think of him as a noisy questioner, but if the Platonic picture is at all correct, Socrates was a great listener, a better listener than a talker. His responses to what his opponents said show this. He was brooding over things. This is a good description of good teaching: brooding, almost in the literal sense, the way a hen broods over her chickens.

50

The Teacher As Brooder

WOFFORD: Why is this good teaching?

BUCHANAN: I think teaching is primarily the business of listening to the pupil and responding to whatever happens in the pupil with further questions, and it could be the questions are statements. I mean statements are questions if you understand them properly—they're proposals to entertain something. A statement is saying, "Well, what do you think of this?" Then when you hear what they think of this, you try some more. Jacques Maritain's book on education is one of the best statements I've heard about what a teacher does in this respect. He thinks of a teacher as knowing more than the pupil does, yet in some sense not conveying it but seeing that it is made available to the pupil. The great use of superior knowledge is to understand what the pupil is learning as it is learned. It takes great wisdom to be able to follow a learning pupil sensitively enough to know what the next step is for him, and you don't press the next step. You watch it happen. If it sticks, you help it a bit, but it's not a transmission or an imposition or a filling of a vessel or any of those things. Those are all bad images of the real teaching function: the real one is this penetration of the intelligence, of one intelligence into another.

WOFFORD: Can you make the seminar, a Socratic seminar, the central technique of this when it brings together people who are at different points, learning along different lines? Can you be sensitive to each when they are at so many different levels?

BUCHANAN: This brings back the theme I was mentioning when talking about the way pupils teach each other. One man cannot pay attention to twenty pupils all at the same time. Inevitably he'll miss a good deal.

But if you realize the thing you do with one pupil is affecting all the others, and they begin to be brooding over each other in some way, watching what's going on—you get a very powerful, combined teaching function going. I don't mean this in any soft sense, it's sometimes very tough stuff, very critical. If we realized this in schools and colleges we wouldn't worry so much about large classes and not enough faculty and all that kind of thing, if teaching were really good. It would become a habit of the whole community. Take the breakaway of students now to form their own classes and set up their own little colleges—they're showing this. They're not connecting with the main establishment, but they're confident they can do this. Bad as their education has been, bad as the teaching has been, they've been learning this and think they can do it all by themselves. They probably can up to a point, perhaps much farther than we think.

WOFFORD: Do you put the Socratic seminar at the center of your vision of an educating community?

BUCHANAN: I think I do, yes. I see the same process going on, of course, in all sorts of places. I've been trying recently to re-write the section of *The Public Thing* on the Constitution. I've been trying to describe the legislative, the administrative and the judicial functions, and have tried to come as close as I can to what the intellectual process is in each of those things. They've become different kinds of dialectic. I started out to see if I couldn't demonstrate the necessity of having a separation of powers in these three, and became so interested in the processes themselves.

Take legislation: you have representatives from very different electorates and constituencies, supposedly with different interests and even preconceptions about things, different convictions. Their business is to make a law, a law applicable throughout the society. This means they have to indulge in a drive towards an abstraction that will cover the whole country, beginning with their own special interests. Now the ordinary process that gets described is, of course, that in Congress people dicker with each other and bargain about their interests. But actually if they're going to make a law, they've got to do the other thing. They've got to consider the whole community, and this means a dialectical, dialogical lifting of themselves above their interests into another level altogether. How much this happens in Congress I don't know, but this is the idea of a legislature and it's kind of miraculous that human beings can do this at all.

Looked at in another way, the administrator begins with the law, the general rule, and finds out how this is to be made effective, down the line to the last citizen. The judicial process is a curious combination of these two when they are not really adequate. That is, if you get a general enough law, you lose the individual. And if you apply it, as administrators do, you may do a great injustice. So you have to have a court which will follow this law and the principle of justice that goes with it down to the last individual. These are very difficult intellectual processes, the last one almost impossible. Generalities do damage to individuals, if you don't look out. That's the reason for analogy. Analogies make it possible to come down to very circumstantial things.

WOFFORD: In your experience, when did you first participate in a seminar that really took off?

BUCHANAN: I think it was with the informal groups of Alec Meiklejohn. My fraternity used to do a funny thing with Alec. We didn't do this very often, but about two or three times a year we'd invite him down for a birthday party. We would sit him in the middle of the room and we'd sit around on the floor as well as on the chairs, and wait for him to start a conversation. He'd start asking about some ordinary thing. It was a very

Socratic situation. We would go on and on and on into the night. The things that happened in those groups were really extraordinary. A lot of it was about the college, some subject matter or other was up, and we would argue. But we'd get into the most complicated arguments and he was really a Socratic character on those occasions. He was never bringing doctrine to us at all. This was all our own stuff, we realized in the end. Almost like a court; we were witnesses to something, bringing in the stuff that was to be talked about, and the conversation made this into whatever pattern emerged in the end. He used to do this in his class in logic, but I never took that. We used to hear about it; that's the reason we had him do it on other occasions. On the most informal occasions, at receptions or parties, he would get into an argument with somebody and people would crowd around and listen.

WOFFORD: Where did you come upon other great teaching, and by whom?

BUCHANAN: Not many other people at Amherst. I had an awfully good teacher at Oxford, in 1919. I had A. D. Lindsey as a tutor. His lectures didn't come off, but in tutorial—you wouldn't call him Socratic, he was a moralist fundamentally—he would translate almost anything you wrote for him into a moral problem and we'd sit and discuss this at great length. This was great teaching and he did it with all his tutees.

WOFFORD: What did you study at Oxford?

BUCHANAN: Philosophy. I read Kant. That was a funny thing. I went to Oxford to prepare to go to India. I was going to learn Sanskrit and I thought at Oxford I could study Indian culture and all that kind of thing. This was because I had seen in the booklet about Oxford a picture and a little discourse on the Indian Center. It hadn't said very much but I just assumed that that was a place where such studies went on. It turned out that this was where they stored the records of the India Office. The building was always closed. So I had to reorganize myself. For one term I did Greats. That's their literary humanities course. I read Plato's *Republic* with Lindsey. Then I thought I'd better shift to Kant and so for two years I read Kant. I wrote a thesis which didn't pass. I had to come home early and didn't spend enough time on it. Then I came back and taught in the Amherst High School for a couple of years.

WOFFORD: Why did you come home early?

BUCHANAN: My mother was ill and financially in trouble. I had to come back and take care of her.

WOFFORD: Was she a teacher in your life?

BUCHANAN: Yes. She was a very lively lady. She started a club, with a funny name, the Crescendo Club, a musical term. This was a literary club, the kind you have in little villages. Women got together and read papers to each other on things they'd read and had discussions of certain things.

WOFFORD: Seminars?

BUCHANAN: No, I don't think so. You read a paper; you usually work very hard on it. You do this only once a year, maybe once in two years. It rotates with the membership, and this was the intellectual life of the community. She had other interests that kept me going in a way. She came from a very small town in Canada and there was an intellectual background that may have had some influence—I've never known much about it. My grandfather, her father, apparently was a lecturer on astronomy to little communities across Ontario. It's almost a legend for me. He used to leave when the snow began to fly in the fall, with a stereoptican lantern, with astronomical slides, and didn't come back until Spring. He hated to work on the farm. He had a very large family with sons, which he worked very hard, and he was a man of leisure and learning. Her family had this curious intellectual drive. I don't know how far it went. She had a kind of curiosity herself, that was beyond the rest of them. She left home and went out West where she married my father. I don't know what it was all about. I've wondered about it. These things, I suppose, are circumstances, environments, and so forth, that make all the difference to a youngster. You don't know where influences come from or how it happens, you get curiosities and yens about certain things.

WOFFORD: How do you get that feeling to people who have few, if any, such influences?

BUCHANAN: Well, that's what we were talking about earlier—the Headstart business. This interests me a good deal. The Headstart people seem to me to have made a great discovery. There are families that don't communicate even. Children don't learn to talk to each other. What this must do to the rest of their lives is an awful thought. You meet people you know this is true of. They have never used language or even their reading ability for an intellectual or even a social purpose.

WOFFORD: Were you at Amherst when the final Meiklejohn blowup came?

BUCHANAN: I happened to be there on the occasion. I was in Harvard but came back for the commencement, and was there when the secret sessions of the trustees were going on, with everyone waiting outside for the result. I went to Alec the day after he was fired and told him he'd been a Socrates and now he must be his own Plato.

WOFFORD: John McCloy of your class, later, as chairman of the Trustees, invited him back for a commencement talk, about thirty years afterwards, didn't he?

BUCHANAN: Yes, this was a great occasion. Jack McCloy happened to be another one in my class who was devoted to Alec. He often disciplined the reunioning class when they began making fun of Alec; they'd get out of hand, get a little drunk and go too far. He made the arrangements for inviting Alec back to speak in the chapel, which was the center of the college. Alec had been very unreligious about the chapel. He had read Epictetus and poetry and a whole lot of funny things instead of the Bible, although he read the Bible, too. Jack could do this because he was the President of the Alumni Association and was about to be made chairman of the board.

He introduced Alec as his old teacher and never mentioned the fact that Alec had been President of the College. The chapel was crowded with a rather hostile audience of reunioning alumni, but it was almost completely won over by the performance. The board of trustees had been convened for their regular meeting at 8:00 in the morning instead of ten or eleven in order to go to hear Alec. Alec got up and began by saying, "I'm pleased to know that I can still stir the Board of Trustees from their lethargy."

Possibility

WOFFORD: What did you go to Harvard to do?
BUCHANAN: Philosophy. I'd come back from Oxford, not having got a degree, and taught high school for a year and a half. Although I didn't have any money, was married and had a child, I suddenly decided I was going to Harvard and get a degree in philosophy no matter what. We lived a pretty tough life for several years. I worked at Harvard and did this half time.
WOFFORD: Why were you so set on a degree?
BUCHANAN: Well, at Oxford I had estimated my capacities as fitted to do secondary teaching. So I came back and went into high school teaching very seriously. And I discovered I wasn't fitted for secondary education.

But I did have some pretty persistent gnawing interests in philosophy. The only way to carry on with that was to get a trade union card, as the word was then, a Ph.D. So I went to Harvard. Alec Meiklejohn wrote a recommendation to Hocking and he wrote back: "From what you tell me, Mr. Buchanan has done his original thinking and he needs to be regularized."

WOFFORD: How original was your thinking?

BUCHANAN: Not very. I'd done a suggestive thesis at Oxford, a very short one I had to write fast and get out, but I don't think it was very important.

WOFFORD: I'm somewhat disturbed by the thought that the major lines and ideas that interested me when I was around seventeen or eighteen are in different forms still the major ones I follow, although they have been elaborated a lot since then. Did the major lines you've been following the twenty years I've known you emerge at such an early point?

BUCHANAN: Hard to say. Doing what you're making me do right now makes me put things together in ways I haven't done before. Two or three times I've been surprised at what I've been saying. I suppose if we did this enough, you'd find this was true. I suspect so.

WOFFORD: What happened at Harvard?

BUCHANAN: I was forced to do things for two years that I didn't want to do. But they were very valuable to me, I must say, particularly mathematical logic. I hadn't much sympathy with that but they were awfully good people at Harvard and I got acquainted with them and actually worked for some. I got involved and did a good deal of that on the side with two or three graduate students. This was good for me. This is a funny thing: I've told you about my trip abroad to study George Boole, which grew out of this interest in mathematical logic. I knew about Boole in algebra when I was at Harvard. Then ten years later I was sent abroad to dig up the George Boole stuff and find out all about him. I realized then, as anybody who studies Boole or mathematical logic does, that this could all be put on a machine. I didn't have much interest in doing that, but the computer world has now happened. I could have followed through on Boole and been in the middle of it. But a computer doesn't interest me that much. It interests me only in another way: all the problems it raises. Here was a brave new world arriving and I just didn't follow into it for myself at all.

WOFFORD: Was Whitehead your chief counselor while you were at Harvard?

BUCHANAN: He wasn't there while I was there. I got acquainted with him at the very end. You see, I did my thesis the year after I left, when I was in New York, and went back for my examination. And that year he had come to Harvard. As near as I could make out, the rest of the faculty was about to turn me down.

WOFFORD: What was your thesis on?

BUCHANAN: Possibility. The concept of possibility. It had some of this mathematical logic in it. They showed Whitehead my thesis. He thought it was good. Some of the others didn't understand it. He said, "If you can't understand this, so much the worse for you." He thought very well of it. It happened that it was very close in some parts to the book he was then writing himself, *Science and the Modern World.* He and I became fast friends, and I knew him and Mrs. Whitehead for ten or twenty years.

WOFFORD: Could you state in a few words the theme of your thesis and book, *Possibility*?

BUCHANAN: I don't believe I could state it in small compass. It's an old fashioned style. I had offered seven other titles of different topics to the faculty, and they turned them all down. One of them—the one I really wanted to do—was on tragedy. They said that one of

59

the things a student can do is a systematic study of a concept, and if you'd like to choose one, we'd like to have you do that. What does "possibility" mean? That was the question. I got my lead from Kant. "Conditions for the possibility of experience" is a great phrase of his. You have to have concepts in order to have any experience. The human mind deals with experience in terms of concepts—abstractions. So I did a job on concepts as they play a part in experience first, and then I divided it into esthetic, scientific, and absolute possibility. Most people think of *Possibility* as a very romantic title and it has that content if you want to look at it that way—a romantic version of it meaning all possible worlds. I did a sort of workmanlike job on the thing, and was glad they made me do it, although I was sorry they wouldn't let me take the ones I wanted to do.

WOFFORD: Do you remember the other ones?

BUCHANAN: One was Authority—that would have been a semi-political one. Tragedy and Authority are the ones I remember.

WOFFORD: Do you think we're on the wrong track in the effort to get the idea of service and work and experience in the world incorporated as part of the scheme of higher education, as we've been urging in the Peace Corps? We've been saying that for people to be ready for concepts they have to have some experience. Now you're turning this back on me, saying that to be ready to understand you've had an experience you have to go out with some concepts.

BUCHANAN: I didn't do this. Kant did. Call this a Copernican revolution in philosophy.

WOFFORD: It's a rhythm you want, I guess.

BUCHANAN: Yes, you have to have both. Kant has an aphorism: concepts without intuitions are empty—by intuitions he means sensations in the form of intuitions, time and space and so on—and intuitions without con-

cepts are blind. That's pretty good. This is what experience can do—it blinds you.

WOFFORD: How do you get the mix that awakens
somebody to both?

BUCHANAN: The concepts are what Kant calls a spontaneous activity of the human understanding. They
come in a flash; they come with experience. They don't
come without it but they don't come from it—concepts
never come from experience. In order to deal with experience the mind supplies them spontaneously.

WOFFORD: Michael Rossman and some of the students
engaged in action now are saying that these flashes will
come in action and that education's task is to catch them
and cultivate them.

BUCHANAN: That's the reason I'm with them. But there
is an internal intellectual process that can enhance this
greatly. I mean the cultivation of the liberal arts. Getting
words and figures of speech and concepts straightened
out and understanding them can enhance the experience
no end. And it has to be done reflectively.

WOFFORD: Yet you once asked Rammanohar Lohia
when Gandhi ever reflected, and Lohia's answer was
he reflected every day and in the midst of action.

BUCHANAN: Lohia and I were discussing the Bhavagad
Gita and I was asking, "What about Gandhi on the
active and contemplative life?" Lohia was saying
Gandhi was always active, even when he was fasting.
This is a choice a man makes, two kinds of life. You
can look at contemplation as an activity. A good many
Oriental philosophers and certain Western philosophers
are very strong on this. The highest form of human
activity is contemplation. The most active a human
being can be is to contemplate. This is not agreed to
by all philosophers, of course, but there is a certain kind
of equivalence. That is what Lohia and I were arguing
about. Gandhi in his action was doing the same as an

61

Indian who went up into the mountains to contemplate, only he was doing it in the active form. This is a little difficult to understand fully because this has to do with the will and the intellect. It's a curious dialectic. Duns Scotus was for the will being the fundamental thing; Aquinas was always for being contemplative, speculative; and Bonaventura was a mixture of these. I'm not sure it's a very sensible question, because they're equivalent. That's what Lohia and I were talking about.

II

THE POWERS OF A MAN

[August 29, 1966]
with
Stringfellow Barr

Reason, Emotion and the Computer

WOFFORD: There's the other side of life—the emotional, the non-intellectual side—that some of your critics say you and your education ignore. Maybe what they mean by your being dangerous is that running the intellectual side so high is hard for people to handle if they are not understanding or coping with the other side.

BUCHANAN: This reflects the deep difference between the ancient and the modern view of the intellect. Over a period of perhaps two hundred years, beginning with the British empiricists in philosophy, we have tended to accept the eighteenth century use of the word "intellect." The old psychology divided up human faculties into reasoning, sense-perception, will, emotion, and so forth. These came from Aristotle's distinctions. The powers of the mind are the powers of the man, really, but we've tended to see them as separate agencies. So when you apply them to education you're training this or that faculty. Aristotle, however, was very much concerned with what now would be called "the whole man." He, with Plato before him, went on to try to find out how you deal with the whole man.

What is the whole man? When you define man as a rational animal you are giving a substantial form for the whole man. The "rational" and the "animal" are related in that the rational includes the animal. This means that no matter what a man does the rational permeates his whole being. Our digestion is different because we have a rational soul. Our emotions are under the reason and so are other things, like perception. So if you want to deal with the whole man you must deal with him rationally.

We feel this very much in the way we now are treated by the medical profession. They've specialized enough so that they deal separately with your liver or your hormones or what have you, and we tend to go to specialists to be treated for this or that thing—quite separately from other functions. We resent this, not quite knowing why—we resent the doctor not treating us as reasonable people, as whole men.

This happens not only in medicine but in many other things in our modern life. We treat each other as animals or, lower than that, as things to be pushed around, managed, and so forth, and we forget this Aristotelian notion that if you're dealing between man and man you'd better be reasonable—which would mean taking into account his whole being.

The fact that the rational has been connected with books and languages and mathematics seems to have brought forth this strange idea that if you're reading a book you're not dealing with a man's emotions, or that after you get through reading a book you'd better turn around and say to the author, "How do you feel?," if you want to know about his emotions. This phrase comes out so often now in public discussions. The politician, the teacher, everybody says "I *feel* Vietnam is wrong" or something like that. That is a sign of this whole thing—our artificial separation of the reason and the emotions, and of the fear of the intellect, as well. But a thing like mathematics is a highly emotional exercise of the mind. The emotions may be cool in one sense but they run very high. This is a kind of ecstasy that is to be found in any form of intellectual work.

The rational soul is leading and controlling—not in the sense of disciplining but in the sense of realizing completely what the whole nature of man is. So if you're educating anybody the channel, the medium, by which you do this will be rational. And you'll have as a result a refining of emotion. Perhaps even—this is more doubtful—you will have a better physiology in general because you've had this rational exercise.

WOFFORD: Freudian psychoanalysis should be rational in that sense?

BUCHANAN: Yes, Freud is very classical on this. He didn't give quite enough play to the reason, perhaps because he thought of it as a sort of super-ego, a kind of conscience or something moral.

WOFFORD: But ultimately the purpose is to get down to a deep understanding of one's self. He also suggests that these deep layers in the human being need to be understood before the reasoning process is going to be very good. Does this mean if you go as far in the world of ideas as you propose, you need psychoanalysis?

BUCHANAN: This brings up a problem that's fascinated me for years. It came to a sort of crisis when I was abroad doing work on George Boole. At the same time I was seeing followers of Mrs. Boole, who had anticipated some of Freud's points in connection with mathematics. I was also concerned about the history of the liberal arts. I used to state the problem this way: If a person were a real liberal artist, if he'd had a real liberal education, why couldn't he psychoanalyze himself? This has been a problem psychoanalysts have been interested in. Why is it necessary to have someone outside you do this for you? Can't you work through your reason, through your subconscious? Then, later, a friend of mine, Erik Erickson, who is a Freudian and trained by Freud himself for a time, pointed out that Freud psychoanalyzed himself and this was the discovery of psychoanalysis. It is very interesting but not a solution because this is still a mysterious thing that Freud did to himself. But it makes a point: Freud had very much the Aristotelian view. The fact that people get sick and have to have a doctor doesn't change this very much. Put it another way: perhaps dialectic is a necessary part of this. This would mean that someone else has to play the reasoning game with you, perhaps on the level of the couch in the clinical office. As you were saying, the psychoanalytic technique is a rational technique; it's trying to understand yourself.

WOFFORD: The story of your education is in large part one of self-dialectic, and yet you prescribe as the center of the learning process, generally, the seminar. What about T Groups sponsored by the National Training Laboratory people? They are sort of applying the seminar approach to the Freudian field.

BUCHANAN: It's a puzzle, what the group therapy people are doing. It's a special use of the rational part of the soul and the mutual understanding is a part of the internal process itself. Plato makes this point that after you've learned the dialectical arts they become internalized and you do this with yourself. But it's only after you've done it externally that it becomes internalized.

STRINGFELLOW BARR: Could I interrupt?

BUCHANAN: Please. You're always welcome.

BARR: I don't want to throw you off this track but I

thought when Harris asked you about the accusation that this intellectual education somehow produces rationalism in the bad sense, a disjunction with the emotional life, you replied that the intellect is tied to the emotions. I was sorry you didn't go one step further—a step perhaps implicit in the word "tied"—and say the intellect frees the emotions.

BUCHANAN: I meant that by the word "related."

BARR: And they get tangled if they're not freed.

BUCHANAN: This is no different from having the rational part get tangled, which is very common. That is, the whole Socratic business is a straightening out of the rational powers. And this means that as you straighten out the rational powers you release emotion more fully than before. The rational powers are the mediums through which the emotions express themselves.

WOFFORD: Jack Seeley would say the reverse is also true: if you can understand or order your loves and hates this will free reason for clear communication.

BUCHANAN: He's given away his case when he says "understand." If you understand your emotions you do it with reason and that is what straightens them out.

WOFFORD: But his argument is that a seminar of ideas doesn't by itself do the whole job of helping you to understand emotions.

BUCHANAN: Well, of course, the seminar is not a panacea. The seminar is in a context. Even at St. John's, we had the context of the other disciplines, and also the context of a very lively community of human beings who were going through all sorts of changes. There is nothing quite as extraordinary as a genuine liberal education making over youngsters. There's a great change not merely in "character" as they used to say in the old days but in the whole psychological makeup of a person. These are the signs that education has taken place. And there may be explosions of these emotions, with people taking pains to turn around and analyze them, too, as Jack Seeley wants done. I think the question now about education is whether we have to turn to this wholly for a time, because we're so disordered. One could have predicted that our education was leading to something like this.

It may be we just have to turn ourselves into therapeutic communities at present, and see what we can do about this disorder we're involved in.

WOFFORD: Another way some students are putting it, when they lose their cool, is that man is a loving animal as well as a learning animal, and that love has dried up on the campuses. You don't find many people who really love ideas or love people or love the earth.

BARR: Yes, but then there aren't too many lovable ideas on the campus.

BUCHANAN: There is a Thomistic doctrine on this that's interesting. Charity, the highest form of love, includes all the other forms, as Dante shows in *The Divine Comedy*. Charity is a very special so-called theological virtue, and its seat is in the intellect. We often talk of the "heart" or something like this, not knowing what we mean by it. But actually the seat of love—all kinds of love—is the intellect. And this means that on any level you want to take love, you're involving a rational soul. But I don't know whether we can really recover this ancient view. The trouble here is with the word "rational." "Rational" has been identified with a part of what the ancients saw as rational, and that is demonstration or discursive thought used in language and mathematics to demonstrate and prove things.

BARR: Syllogistic stuff—slightly "computerish"?

BUCHANAN: It all can be computed. This kind of thought can be put on machines. The human mind, the mind of the programmer, will still have to work, perhaps even harder, to get it in that form. But *his* operation will be of another kind—intellectual intuition: insight. That is the essential rational power. Proofs and discoursive thought are a secondary kind of reason. Now most modern psychologists, and even philosophers, think of reason as being merely that kind of mechanical thing, which, of course, is loosed from the emotions in one sense, although not really even then. This connects again because all this can be made into poetry. The great mathematical works following Newton, those which put together his whole calculus in the field of mathematical physics and astronomy, have been called mathematical poems. They have that power, that quality, if you read them properly, to make the emotions run high, too.

BARR: In defense of the contemporary view isn't it also true that this computerizing, rationalizing, syllogizing mechanical process, though it can be turned to poetry, can also be a place you hide from insights? It seems to me that's where this ugly sense of rationalism comes from. A guy goes off and does this kind of business, and thereby avoids love, insight, anything that computers can't do for him.

BUCHANAN: This is embodied now in what the rebel students call "the establishment." The university, the academy, has become almost wholly devoted to this mechanical reasoning. Specialization has done this—the writing of theses, and all that kind of thing. There is an opaqueness to this that means real alienation. Put it another way, the computers may teach us this. The computers can write better Ph.D. theses than we can. And they'd probably better do it and let us do something more constructive.

This is true of undergraduate education in a very acute way. If you let the research kind of reason come into the undergraduate life, you get a very dangerous thing. This is true of your professions. Modern professions are pretty nearly computerized. And if you bring that into undergraduate teaching you will stultify the whole thing. This has already gone very far anyway—this invasion of the graduate school into the liberal arts college in such a way that nothing is left of the real live intellectual arts.

WOFFORD: My thought would be you need to get the professions down into the undergraduate school, not to train lawyers or doctors or priests for those specialties but primarily to teach the aspects of those professions which everybody ought to know.

BUCHANAN: You have me split there. I'm trying to think about this.

BARR: Reverting to Harris's question about whether there aren't people who would say, "Well, that seminar thing does a lot of this, but it leaves you with nobody to love, no ideas to love." It seems to me the seminar when it's at all successful is provoking loving insight. Getting you in a corner, Socratically, is part of it, I admit a very important part, but it's not at all rationalistic in the nineteenth century sense. I saw more love in seminars than I'd seen for some time because the material they were reading, a lot of it, is loving. You can't love when you really can't tell what they're talking about. It's a very queer business. My friend Cicero reads these dialogues of Plato and gets nothing out of them except the love—in the form of rhetoric, of course. He doesn't even get the intellectual insights. But Cicero has something on his side there: he's saying, "My God, how he writes!" Plato invites us both to love and to know in some integrated way.

BUCHANAN: Yes.

BARR: Not just to know coldly.

BUCHANAN: And, of course, if you take some of the more recent readings of Plato—and this was clear even in Jowett in the old days—Socrates is a lover all the way through in an almost literal sense. The whole question of homosexuality among the Greeks pervades the dialogues and is a clarifying thing—a straightening out of all those affective relations which now you'd treat as if they were diseases.

The Weight of Experience

WOFFORD: Perhaps there is a difference between a seminar laid down in the midst of conventional education, which catches the students somewhere in sixteen years of constant classroom education, in the "endless catacombs of formal education" as Kingman Brewster said, a seminar for people who have not been out in the world, who may not have even had time to catch their breath enough to love anybody or much of anything, a seminar for people who've had so little experience; and the Socratic dialogues we're talking about, where the people are walking in from a battle, or from the marketplace, or from a love affair. The student rebellion in this country is asking whether academia doesn't need to join with them out in the world. A seminar with people who come in from the civil rights front or from the Peace Corps might come alive much more easily than a seminar of freshmen who have been in classrooms for twelve or fourteen years.

BUCHANAN: My experience with the seminar illustrates this point in another way. While I was at the People's Institute Mortimer Adler suggested we take the Columbia Honors Course, which was run on the seminar plan, and do it for adults. We did it in New York public libraries. This experience with adults was my first real introduction to the more systematic of the dialectical forms. I realized there was something very slow about adult seminars, very much slower than with the young students I had had before. This was a bit puzzling. You thought, "These people aren't able to learn." Those were the days when psychologists were trying to find out if people could still learn anything when they were forty years old. Of course, they found they could learn much more than they do when they're young. Then I realized—and rather fully and vividly—that when you're doing an adult seminar you are pulling big weights of experience with every word you use. It's a massive thing that's taking place with adults, whereas with youngsters it's light and gay and kind of wonderful.

BARR: Puppyish.

BUCHANAN: Adults seldom will do this, unless you get people that are slightly schizophrenic or something. It's nice to have one or two of those in a seminar, as a matter of fact. I did a seminar at the Riggs Clinic at Stockbridge, Massachusetts for one year in which they were all schizophrenics. It was a wonderful experience, absolutely wonderful—but quite different from what I was doing at the same time with some adults in Pittsfield, people of middle age, and bourgeois. Oh, God, that was a tough business. But when you'd done it, you had done a remarkable thing. That is, you had made the rational (if you want to use that word here about it) penetrate a whole depth of life and these people were much more educated than youngsters are.

BARR: Shouldn't you postscript that though? You were not only pulling a heavy weight of experience which turned out to be worth pulling; you were also up against some frozen, vested interests that the kids didn't have. And while it was eminently worthwhile helping them get rid of those vested interests that kept them from thinking, some of the excitement of the kids was that they had fewer of those dragging at them. I think the

72

fact the adult had suffered certain things gave him the superiority you imply he had over the kid. But he had also sometimes declined to suffer, and closed doors the kid hadn't yet closed.

WOFFORD: I wasn't proposing postponement of higher education till middle age. The Socratic model often consisted of young men. But they were seminars that took place in the midst of life, in the midst of action, and this is part of what the student movement is now saying to higher education: join us or let us construct our own seminars on the firing line—wherever it is, overseas or at home. Or let us go out and try the world, and then come in ready for a Socratic seminar.

BUCHANAN: You're right. We forget it sometimes: Socrates went to the marketplace to do this, the gymnasiums, and everywhere else.

BARR: I'm always moved by his going to the marketplace; but I'm also moved by what sounds to me—in his proposal for the education of the guardians—like getting enough time and enough seclusion to really reflect. It seems to me that Socrates is saying that the marketplace experience helps you to think if you do the right thing with it. But I think Socrates would be alarmed by how much marketplace there is in the life of an American. It's a funny marketplace, not quite the Athenian marketplace. There are an awful lot of commercial plugs in the American's heart and I'm not sure how much they help him.

BUCHANAN: But you remember how much of a city man he was. Remember how unhappy he was when he went outside the city walls?

BARR: Yes, but this is an old quarrel between you and me. Socrates thought that five thousand was the right population for a city. You put him in Manhattan and see what he says.

WOFFORD: Earlier you saw a sequence of Man, God,

and the World in history. The Greeks were focusing on Man, the Middle Ages on God, and now we were coming to the World.

BUCHANAN: You've got this out of order. My history is incompetent—I can do this because I don't know much history—but I put it the other way: the ancient world, up to the Middle Ages, philosophically and culturally, was concerned about God.

WOFFORD: Including Socrates?

BUCHANAN: Yes. The upward dialectic was very strong. That is, they were seeking the top of this. This was even true of the Romans, and certainly of the medievals. But at the time of the Renaissance the concern shifted to man, and that's been going on now for about three hundred years. The proper study of man has been mankind. And now—this is my strong hunch—we are concerned about comprehending the world. We're only beginning to do it, and it's upsetting us pretty badly. As a matter of fact, the Renaissance was pretty badly upset when it began studying man. It found a volcano there. Well, we've found pandemonium, an unmanageable chaos almost, when we try to think of the world. This is on all sorts of levels—political, economic, religious. Man is being exploded into a thousand fragments. Existentialism shows this. But the world is what we're working at. We haven't got very far with it—don't know what to do with it.

WOFFORD: Is the existentialist view—which I think is the predominant view among the young people we've been talking about—stretching for the world? Or does it seek justification of everything in terms of man-to-man relations, direct encounter with another human being, an act that is immediately justifiable: feeding a child, tending a sick person.

BUCHANAN: It's a little puzzling here. The other day the young staff member who wrote a paper on the

Civilization of the Dialogue opened our discussion with a quotation from Pico della Mirandola's essay called "The Dignity of Man." It's what we used to call at St. John's a small great book. The paragraph was very existential. It was saying man can choose to be anything, and he can partake in, become a part of, anything he wants to—he can go and become a beast; he can become a god; he can do anything. Sartre, Camus and the people like that are saying this but it was a curious thing to read because there it was in the Renaissance. Here it was, out of the sixteenth century or thereabouts as if it had been written yesterday by an existentialist. Of course there was a Renaissance style to it.

BARR: It was a beautiful thing.

BUCHANAN: Yes. The existentialists, it seems to me, are reporting (I'm prejudiced here when I say this, but this is what I think about it) the kind of ragged end of the study of man. They're saying there's nothing left of him. Della Mirandola was saying there's everything left of him. The existentialists are reporting the explosion of the object of their central attention, and I'm saying that the world is taking over as the object. You won't find the existentialists saying this. They will tell you, "Yes, man will build his own world," but they're not emphasizing the word "world" there. It's in politics, economics and the great topics that you get the scheme of the world coming through. The youngsters are talking about this when they talk about cross-cultural experiences—as they do in the Peace Corps.

BARR: Yes, but when Harris listed their concerns there was one missing: Vietnam. Or isn't this one? I keep hearing it is.

WOFFORD: Certainly.

BUCHANAN: Vietnam is a curious, fumbling, feeble attempt to get ahold of the world, because everybody knows that Vietnam is in some sense enmeshed deeply in the whole world. There isn't any solution short of some kind of a world order. I think everybody knows this.

BARR: On the other hand, in justice to Harris's account on behalf of these kids, Vietnam is added to the list not so much as an interesting case of statecraft; it's more: "I saw a baby crying."

BUCHANAN: Yes.

BARR: "And I'm against it!"

WOFFORD: The other recognition coming from a lot of people is that you find the world everywhere. You don't have to find the world far away. Take a problem—the city or the slum or racial discrimination—and a student who goes out to the slums of Oakland or into Harlem, or into suburbia, who goes across this cultural frontier, is discovering the world, because he's got another foothold in it; he's got another angle of vision on it. That's what Peace Corps volunteers feel strongly when they come back: that it's just as much "going out into another world" when they go to city hall here, or to a slum here, as it was overseas.

BARR: Martin Luther King's insistence that Vietnam was connected with the Civil Rights Movement infuriated the press. They kept advising: "Don't talk about the world! Stick to your problem!"

BUCHANAN: This is the form in which I see the world emerging. That is, the individual young student now is saying, "I don't belong to the Establishment because it's provincial, it's outworn, it's got to be broken up!" But what he's really saying is this: "I and the Establishment, too, belong to something bigger and we've got to find that bigger object." When you go to the slum, or to another culture, you are seeing it as another part of something. It isn't just the slum in itself that you're interested in; you're trying to find what it belongs to in the way of a larger object. I may be wrong about this.

WOFFORD: And the way you personally found this larger object, the world, was a long, long route through the great books?

BUCHANAN: Well, I have to say I don't know how this ever happened to me.

India, Wilson and the World

WOFFORD: You were resisting the journey, according to your account, for a long time.

BUCHANAN: Yes, going back to my reason for going to Oxford. Remember, I was going to be Indian the rest of my life. I wanted to get in a world or in a culture or in a something or other which was whole. I wanted to get the world put together in some way, and I thought India was the place where this might happen. As Arnold Toynbee puts it, the counter radiations from India were getting to be strong in this country. It seemed to me it was very important for somebody—I wasn't thinking of a peace corps or anything like that at the time; that is, not a movement of students doing this—*I* was going to do it. I was going to spend my life there seeing what you could get going between the two worlds. As always when I go abroad, I find I'm very American and have to come home. But as soon as I get home I feel the other way; I want to get back again. All my life I've felt this.

WOFFORD: Was this part of Wilson's appeal to you?

BUCHANAN: Very much. I think I discovered the world with Wilson, insofar as I discovered it. It was a kind of a weak affair, now that I look back on it, but it meant everything to me. You know, for a short time Wilson was the great symbol in the world for this. He represented the world.

BARR: I didn't realize you'd had this Indian disease quite so deep. In my case I hadn't contracted the Indian fever in those days at Oxford—it came very late in life—but as a youngster before I'd ever been out of this country I had the European fever. I still feel that people who try to write American history with no discernible comprehension of European culture are up against a very funny thing—it's like writing the history of the west end of an Oklahoma town, or something. It's too small a focus to get light on. But I didn't know you were literally thinking you might spend your life in India.

BUCHANAN: Oh yes, I was set to do that.

WOFFORD: But you came back and spent your life for a long long time in Kant and Aquinas and Plato.

BUCHANAN: Yes. What Winkie's saying is relevant here: I perhaps substituted Europe for it for a time being, although I never had the attachment to Europe that Winkie had. For five years after I got back from Oxford I was hell-bent to get back to Europe; but definitely I wouldn't have been interested in the Rhodes scholarship unless I had thought of it as being a way to train myself to go to India.

If I remember right, I was one of sixteen final candidates for the Rhodes scholarship from Massachusetts. It was pretty tough competition. There were people from Harvard, and I thought, Who was I to be up against these people who had a better education than I'd had, and everything else? So I took it very simply and just talked to the committee (the president of Harvard, the head of Groton, and as a matter of fact the dean of Amherst, who was pretty skeptical about me). When they asked me why I wanted to go I told them a rather long story of why I wanted to go to India, and they were impressed. Lowell was interested in me because I ran the one and two mile on the track team and that's what he'd done, but he was impressed also by the India story. I think I was chosen because of this. Then the India Institute at Oxford turned out to be just the warehouse for storing the Indian Office records and Sanskrit was not even taught at Oxford. There was nothing of India at all at Oxford—nothing at all.

WOFFORD: It was World War II that brought you back to the idea of the world as the central point of view?

BUCHANAN: Yes, and your Foundation for World Government did it, too. I had also read Toynbee, you have to remember. Toynbee does things to you. He was what I'd been looking for always, I guess. I hadn't fallen for Spengler or any of the other world historians, but Toynbee had me caught right away, partly on account of style. But also the idea that he had seemed to me remarkable. You know his question: "What is the intelligible object of history?" He starts with the nation and sees that can't be it; he moves to a civilization but that finally isn't it; and before he gets through with the ten volumes, he's saying, "It's got to be a world religion that comprehends this."

It's an internal dialectic with himself, and with his subject matter, that made him go in that direction. It's Toynbee, I suppose, more than anything else that fills in my question about the world. That is, he's come the closest to trying to do it of anyone. I realize he's failed in many respects, but the spirit of the man and the accomplishment are very great, it seems to me.

WOFFORD: What are the other milestones on this road that led you back to the idea of the world, or opened it up for you?

BUCHANAN: We haven't talked about what the first world war did to my generation. I don't know how many other people were with me on this but for me that war was somehow a world catastrophe. I don't mean just in the sense that it blew up a lot of buildings and killed a lot of people and moved a lot of populations. But

79

in some sense the world became uncommunicative, as a whole, at that point, and it's gotten worse. Nothing has improved this.

I realize you can give an optimistic picture about communications and science and all this kind of thing, but the more these are loaded on the worse the communications get, from my point of view. Human beings just haven't ever pulled themselves together again. Now there may be a great illusion in this—they probably weren't pulled together before. But my world was. My world felt solid before the war. Probably a very provincial and small world, but my world was broken and this was true of the worlds of other provincial people. I haven't known how to put it together and I haven't seen anyone who knows how to put it together since. That's the reason I admire Toynbee so much. He was going to do this or bust! And perhaps he did bust. But he tried very hard to do it. Of course the League of Nations and Wilson's tragic career in connection with that impressed me very much as a dramatic spectacle. But it was saying the same things in a very vivid and deep way.

I remember when I went to Oxford I had an evening before I sailed with an old Amherst friend of mine. And I made up an expression—it's sentimental and perhaps a little silly—but I said to him: I'm going abroad to view the embers of the world. I've never amended that judgment.

III

BARR ON BUCHANAN: FUNNY STUFF

[August 29, 1966]

Virginia v. *New England*

WOFFORD: Now that Scott has gone let me ask you a few questions. I started by leveling the charge at Scott—or delivering the compliment to him—that his students and critics see Socrates in him, and he has been denying that, more or less. Then you came into the conversation sort of like Alcibiades did at the end of the *Symposium.* So let me get you talking about him.

BARR: I met Scott in 1919 when both of us were Rhodes scholars at Balliol College, Oxford. Balliol had had as its master a few decades earlier Benjamin Jowett, the translator of Plato, the translation Scott first read. I came there very differently from Scott. He came with his consuming interest in India; I came with a consuming interest in England. Scott was brought up in a New England dissenter tradition, religiously and intellectually; I was brought up in the Virginia assenting tradition as far as England was concerned. (My father was dean of the cathedral in New Orleans.)

WOFFORD: Did you know then that Scott was a conscientious objector?

BARR: No, I don't recall its being discussed. It was a
complicated case.

WOFFORD: He finally decided his conscientious objection had to be contained within military service.

BARR: There again we were different. Typically, I had
volunteered in 1917, but I had very bad fallen arches.
At Virginia I tried out for football and crumpled up
like a caterpillar in the sun. I couldn't do much of
anything, except ride a horse. But Woodrow Wilson had
convinced me that this was it, and except for this absurd
physical disability which kept me out of the infantry
I had every reason for volunteering. Our Government
had asked the French whether there was anything we
could do immediately while building an army, and they
said, "Yes, send an ambulance corps." So we got up
an ambulance corps. I went up to Allentown, Pennsyl-
vania, where we were trained, but I didn't last in the
Ambulance Corps because they didn't have enough
gasoline and started twenty mile hikes, and of course
I crumpled again, and was transferred to a sitting job
for the duration.

When I got to England in 1919, the world was not
in embers for me. Not merely because I have a more
sanguine temperament than Scott has, but because I was
less sensitive to the implications of a great many events
that were going on in the world. And in England and
later in France, where I spent most of my vacations—
partly out of infatuation for the French language, which
I wanted to master—I found means of communicating
that I didn't have with most Americans. They seemed
to see life much more as I saw it. This is not a unique
experience for Southerners in Europe, my generation
of Southerners, at least. We knew the Civil War had
been lost and could communicate with Europeans with

fewer strains than with Northern or Western Americans—not because of any clash over Appomattox, but because the Northerner seemed to us rather infantile, or at least the optimism of the United States proper struck us as infantile. Toynbee would write many years later that the Southerner didn't see the world the way other Americans did because he had known overwhelming defeat and military occupation, and this meant that he had had a community experience of a sort most Europeans had had and that most Americans just couldn't envisage. I mean, we Americans win wars; we don't lose them! So I collided with Scott. College hadn't opened. We'd come over a little early, which is against regulations. When I met him I was dazed. I had never met anybody like that. I very soon then encountered the Socratic question. I'd read at least two Platonic dialogues, the *Apology* and the *Crito,* because you couldn't get into Oxford without passing examinations in Greek, Latin, and mathematics—and I'd chosen the *Apology* and *Crito* for my text; and I certainly would have thought of myself as a great admirer of Socrates. But what I didn't understand in those dialogues would fill a dictionary. And here this man kept raising funny questions. I didn't really know what he was at for a good while. And then some of the questions were so probing that in the first two or three weeks of our acquaintance I decided probably we'd do well to avoid each other. He felt too prickly. He wasn't prickly; he was very gentle but these damnable questions were always interfering with my notion of social intercourse. Probably for a week or ten days I may have succeeded in avoiding Scott, but then we got back together and I got absolutely fascinated by his mind. I'd never encountered one like it.

WOFFORD: You've been doing that all your life since then, separating in irritation and meeting again.

BARR: Oh, yes! Later in life when I came to know Plato better I realized Scott was the most Socratic man I had known. And through him I met the second most Socratic man I had known, Alexander Meiklejohn, who was in England on a year's leave of absence from Amherst, and *he* started some of these questions. By this time, though, I saw what the game was a little bit better. And during that period in Oxford one or two young Englishmen got fascinated by this and started what was in effect a sort of seminar—we weren't reading the so-called great books, but we were discussing various problems, and there was a little coterie formed around Scott, mostly British. I'm not sure that I wasn't the only other American besides Scott. And I slowly began to hear this Socratic tune.

Then there developed a queer kind of intimacy. We differed on nearly everything; some of this was New England vs. Virginia, some of it was philosopher vs. God-knows-what. I went over there thinking I was going to read English literature, but at a certain point I was very unhappy in my work. And I discussed a shift from English literature with Scott who said, "Well, from the way you talk I think you're a historian. I don't think you want to be a literary critic or anything of that sort. Your real interest, it seems to me, is historical. Have you considered trying to get permission to switch to the School of Modern History?" I had half-way considered this, but unfortunately I'd had a painful experience in history: the only course I ever flunked in my whole life was history—at Tulane when I was a freshman, a poisonous course. I finally said, sort of desperately, "I've got a tutorial coming up Friday. I'm going to write a paper designed to please the tutor, and if it does please him, I'm going to stop studying English Literature because this is too ridiculous." So I wrote the paper and the tutor said it was wonderful. I immediately went to the Master at Balliol and asked him if I could change to History. He said, "Well, yes, if you don't make a habit of it, like Henry VIII." So I shifted over to History.

Then during the rest of the time that Scott was at Oxford (he left earlier than I) I used to discuss with him the history I was studying and writing about. I remember particularly the French Revolution and Napoleon, the principal period I was studying. I used to argue about Napoleon with him, and he was always, of course, very original in his views, very unorthodox, always apologetic and saying, "I don't know anything about this, but . . ." Finally, when I was getting toward the oral examinations some of my friends who had heard my views on Napoleon urged me to smother them or I'd flunk. I did not smother them and I was congratulated on the original views. I neglected to point out that they'd really originated in Scott's mind.

Later I saw him very briefly when I visited this country in 1921. I went to Amherst and spent a day or so with him, then back to Europe for a year in Paris and a year in Brussels. During that time we corresponded some, but not regularly. I came back to this country and taught at the University of Virginia in the school of history for twelve years. About the fifth or sixth year I was teaching there, all of a sudden the head of the philosophy department accosted me and asked what I knew about Scott Buchanan. It turned out they were considering him for an Associate Professorship. I said, "He's the most remarkable man I've ever met, but he's not an easy person, and I would rather not urge his appointment. It would mean a great deal to me personally to have him here, but I would rather not urge an appointment because you might find him a very difficult customer to handle." They decided to risk it and got him. Well, they recognized his superb teaching powers, but there were lots of little ructions—

his Socratic nature disturbed them as well as it had me and others.

During the years we were in Charlottesville we saw a great deal of each other. Certain questions he raised shifted my teaching rather sharply. My teaching had been in large lecture courses, but I got up a section of the course and read great historical works with them—Herodotus, Thucydides, Plutarch. I began to see why Scott was hipped on the great books. I'd read some of these books before, of course, some of them partly in Greek, but I didn't really get the point of any of them. I suppose one never does, it's all relative—but certainly I didn't. Slowly Scott got me to understand why they had such extraordinary effects or had had for him and Adler and McKeon and various people in the New York effort he'd been involved in.

I was ripe enough so that when Bob Hutchins tried to get Scott and me to the University of Chicago to serve on his Committee on the Liberal Arts, to try to find out what had happened to the undergraduate curriculum in this country, I was terribly troubled. I didn't want to go, I had an enormous and deep attachment to the university I was teaching in—my alma mater—and I'd been very happy teaching there. During that period, incidentally, I'd edited the *Virginia Quarterly Review* for three years, and Scott was constantly arguing about that. Finally, I decided I didn't want to go. I remember a conversation—Mortimer Adler was there. Scott and he twisted my wrist for about two hours, and finally Mortimer said, "I've got a question. You say you're interested in history and want to teach history and you don't want to go to the University of Chicago and don't feel philosophically fitted for the task that we want to undertake, and we are philosophers and you aren't. Just answer one question and I'll let you alone." It was more than one question—Scott had some too—but it came to this: "Which do you care most about, history or truth?" I knew what he meant, and said, "The truth, of course." And then I said, "Oh, go to hell! I'll come, I guess. But I'm only going on a year's leave." This disgusted Scott, and he said, "Now don't put your foot in the water that way. You're not going to find out what the water's like unless you dive." And I said, "Well, I'm not going to find out what the water's like then, because I'm going to put my foot in."

I got a year's leave and said I would see what this was all about, and particularly whether it was my dish of tea. Scott's probably told you the sequel in Chicago. For me it was a very peculiar experience. I got excited by the seminar that Scott was running. I think the crucial things that happened to me were the reading of two books, the dialogues of Plato, and we read all of them, and Euclid's elements of geometry. These two books had such a profound effect on me that when St. John's came up I think it's truthful to say that if I hadn't read those two books I wouldn't have done it. I accepted the presidency of St. John's because I felt if those books could do that for me they could do it for the dumbest freshman in America. They had so much dynamite in them, intellectually.

WOFFORD: How do you measure the dynamite of the books versus the dynamite of the Socratic process?

BARR: It's hard to separate, isn't it? I'll put it this way: I can't imagine the books having packed that dynamite if I'd read them alone. In meeting and discussing them there was tremendous excitement. I was even having funny dreams that I think were caused by those two works. You're right—it was the total experience I was persuaded by.

When Scott and I finally, more or less, halfway promised to go to St. John's nobody had ever discussed who the president would be. In fact, I wouldn't have been

87

so interested in St. John's if Richard Cleveland, who was the moving spirit in the Board, hadn't talked in Baltimore with us for a whole day without ever mentioning the question of who would be president. This excited me. We were talking about what the College should do and Scott and I were advising them, not talking about accepting jobs, although everybody in the room knew that might occur—but it wasn't relevant: we were talking about the program.

Once Dick Cleveland made up his mind that the program made sense, he asked us whether we'd consider coming, one of us to serve as president. Scott said, "Well, that'll have to be you." Then I said, "I beg to disagree. That would be absurd because the program would be yours. I'm not competent to do that. It would be better for the person handling the program to be president." And he said, "I couldn't do that because I don't answer my mail." And I said, "Yes, but that's on principle, not accidental. You don't believe in answering mail." And he said, "No, I don't, but everybody else believes in it, and you would answer it."

WOFFORD: That's probably true, isn't it?

BARR: Yes, that was true. I laughed, and I said, "Well, I'll accept the presidency on condition—and only on condition—that you will be dean." And he said, "Oh, my God, I don't want to be a dean." I said, "Well, I just finished telling you I don't want to be a college president. And I've now told you on what terms I'll go." So he said, "All right." And we went. By this time we had had a relationship for several years that made it easier to work out the division of labor.

During those years, I used to tease Scott by saying I translated him to his public, and I added that I realized I miss the point but at least I make intelligible what I do say. I think Scott knew this was right because I would necessarily be held responsible by the public in a way he wouldn't be, and it was clear he could handle the educational stuff going on on campus in a way I couldn't hope to.

WOFFORD: Some of your friends would say that but for Scott and his books and his damned Socratic questions you would have been president of the University of Virginia or Senator from Virginia—that Scott was a destroyer in your life.

BARR: Yes, a lot of them felt that. The Spirit That Denies was one of our colleague's names for him. People who knew me and were fond of me and weren't fond of Scott made that kind of statement about him. On the other hand, you have to remember the rest of the story is people like Bob Hutchins and Mortimer Adler and Dick McKeon wondering why in the hell he was so attached to me. They could see why I was attached to him but they didn't see what I supplied to Scott that he needed.

WOFFORD: How would you compare your two educations? What was his like when you met him at Oxford?

BARR: I think the presence of Alec Meiklejohn at Amherst did extraordinary things to Scott. He was almost the only college president of his time who was really completely alive intellectually. One in a generation is probably a goodly number. But he was also getting very exciting people on his faculty. Scott was encountering some very interesting minds. Amherst was an exciting place in those years. Alec was always playful about this: "How could I have affected you? You didn't pay any attention to me."

The University of Virginia at that period—just before World War I—was a very different kettle of fish. The University had no funds to speak of, like everything in the South in that period. But the University had—and Scott later agreed with this judgment, I think—some extraordinary, unique, rich personalities on its faculty.

They were a little eccentric, if you like, a little more like Oxford actually, in teaching and in what they thought life was about. Scott was, I think, genuinely intrigued by Charlottesville. He considered it a foreign country and acted accordingly and was kind of terribly amused by it.

When I met Scott I had never really been awakened intellectually. I'd been too uncritical of the school and university systems of my generation. I'm afraid I was kind of a "good boy." Except for that famous history course, I'd got good grades and liked the work. But I don't think anything really happened to me until Oxford, and the realest thing that happened to me at Oxford was Scott.

The Socratic Game

WOFFORD: When you say "Scott was the most Socratic" and Alec Meiklejohn the second most "Socratic," what exactly do you mean?

BARR: I mean the Socratic question, which I think is very ill-understood in our society. The dialectical question aims at helping you examine your expressed opinions and see whether they are wind-eggs—empty. A lot of mine turned out full of wind. This is a very special talent which I think we succeeded in cultivating to a rather remarkable degree at St. John's. It was our chief teaching instrument. During those years we were supposed to be "Thomistic," because St. Thomas was on our list—and Aristotelian—and because of Thomas we were supposed to be crypto-Catholic, and by an extension probably Fascists because we were therefore authoritarian. We'd ask, why were we authoritarian? Because we didn't have the elective system—we told people what they were going to study if they attended college there. This misapprehension amused me because, thanks to Scott, if any label was to be put on the college, it was Platonic, or Socratic, and certainly not Aristotelian. There were several ardent Aristotelians on the faculty, but then I consider it highly Platonic to insist on having some Aristotelians around, whereas I do not think it's Aristotelian to have some Platonists.

WOFFORD: You said you caught onto the game of the Socratic question. Let me ask you what the critics of Scott, and maybe of Socrates, always ask: "Is it a game?" That is, his profession of ignorance—that he knows he doesn't know, but that he's puncturing the pose of those who think they know—is that genuine? Or does he daze you because he knows so much?

BARR: No. I think he dazed me like the stinging fish in Socrates. He dazed me because before I talked very long with him I made a fool of myself. I have enough vanity to find this a disagreeable experience.

WOFFORD: What's the fish?

BARR: I forget how it's generally translated; cuttlefish, stingray, or something. It's a fish that paralyzes you. Socrates was accused of paralyzing by his questions.

WOFFORD: Torpedo fish?

BARR: Yes, torpedo fish. I don't take the charge of duplicity or deception very seriously. I think what Socrates was trying to do was deeply sincere—to use a rather flabby word. He sincerely wanted to know the truth. I think the reason I keep using the word "game" is that the rules of dialectic are not unlike the rules of a game. You ask your question, get the answer and keep asking questions until you find where the argument leads. And too often it leads to a stupid remark and everybody present knows that there's been a reduction to absurdity, like the *reductio* in mathematics, in Euclid.

This seems to me sincere, except that Socrates could

usually (and the same is true of Scott) predict when the wind-egg will be hatched. But I think it's not deceptive, in the sense that both of them admit the possibility that they will be surprised and find that, while you may have expressed yourself a little clumsily, nevertheless what you meant to say is true. The real point of the so-called dialectic is that both of you are seeking the truth, and you do it according to rules, in this case the rules of logic. This is like playing tennis with somebody that you love to play tennis with because every time you play with him your game improves and you enjoy it more. What you want is the excitement of good tennis and not the victory: that's irrelevant.

WOFFORD: But you don't usually want to play tennis with somebody so much worse than you are that it's not a good game. The amazing thing about Scott—

BARR: He's always willing.

WOFFORD: The powerful thing is that he seems always really to believe that inside your dull mind there is something that's going to surprise him.

BARR: I think this is true. Although I insist that sometimes when a good tennis player, out of his condescension, plays with me, he makes me play better. It's true, I pull his game down because I'm not able to return the balls adequately, but he makes me better and this is sort of interesting to him. And now and then I surprise him—I hit a ball he didn't think I could hit. I think Scott, like Socrates, is a born teacher. He's terribly excited if he can cause an insight in another mind. But to that I would append something that I would stick by, and that is: he really believes you may have something. I think Scott has an infinite faith in the human intellect and in the surprising motions of the human intellect. He wouldn't hesitate to say, "Jones is stupid"—not cruelly but just noting the fact. But if you say, "Well, then, why listen to him?" I think he would say, "Because the stupidest people sometimes come out with very good ideas. Sometimes they're too stupid to know they're good, but they come out with them."

So I don't think "deception" really fits the dialectic. That would be a moral judgment on an intellectual process that has great rewards in it. When Socrates is sophistical, he's doing tricks in order to help a person see something. But I don't think he can predict exactly where an argument is coming out, and I think he learns from people less able than he. I'm sure Scott learns from a lot of people who haven't his intellectual power.

WOFFORD: A Buchanan seminar really goes against the whole grain of conventional education, because in the first place he's prepared to mix everybody of all levels of information and intelligence around one table; second, he's willing to operate that kind of a table in a way in which he's not giving out the truth, but is exploring jointly with them.

BARR: Yes.

WOFFORD: In this professional and specialist world, this seems amateurish and superficial.

BARR: Oh, yes. Dilettante. I've met very few men who wouldn't suppose Scott was irresponsible intellectually, because he's freer from intellectual phobia than anybody I've known. He's not afraid. He doesn't claim to know the things he doesn't know, and he doesn't mind exploring them with anybody that'll give him a hand. And he's very suspicious of the specialist who knows "the truth" in his field. He thinks their statements usually don't hold up under examination. And there's no area that the human mind has explored that doesn't interest him. In my own case, while Euclid excited me terribly, by and large mathematics and science don't hold me very much. There's always something I want to do more. They're not only difficult for me but they're not terribly appealing but as you know, they appeal terrifically to Scott. So does medicine, so does law. Anything the mind works on appeals to him.

WOFFORD: Is the case for the Socratic seminar that it teaches a process you can then apply to any problem or any part of life?

BARR: I think so. In the St. John's days, more even than now, this sounded like saying "mind training." People saw red—thought it stupid. The Deweyites called it absurd. But it wouldn't have shocked my father.

WOFFORD: Why wouldn't it have shocked him?

BARR: My father used a phrase then current in his generation that so-and-so is "an educated man," and he didn't mean information. He merely meant that whatever he talks about, he talks about it with wisdom and in the spirit of inquiry. He's not opinionated or dogmatic or frightened. I don't know if he ever asked himself exactly what he meant by "an educated man," but he certainly meant: he can use his mind. Now, the critics of St. John's, some of them, were in effect saying, "There isn't anything you can do to this boy to teach him to use his mind." And I think we regularly did.

Melancholia

WOFFORD: This account of Scott's optimism about the educational process probably ought to be qualified by the other side of him that gives some truth to the charge that he's a destroyer. There is a melancholy side.

BARR: I used to state that case at St. John's by saying that three or four years after our New Program started I was delighted with it and Scott was depressed with it. The difference between Scott and me was that when I see a baby I'm enchanted with him; and Scott is always feeling, "Well, that's not the baby I had in mind.

Babies ought to be better than that." All human enterprises, including birth, seem to him a little disappointing. He's a Platonist in the sense he's got some notion of a baby in the back of his mind that no baby lives up to, whereas to me it's such a miracle the little brat is alive—so what, if he has defects. His ears stick out and he's cross-eyed, certainly, but he's still alive. I don't think Scott and I were really disagreeing on the facts of St. John's at this point as much as that I'm always so impressed by anything coming to life and he's always so disappointed it didn't come to more life—because in fact it is partly alive and partly dead, like my mind.

WOFFORD: Do you understand his tragic view of the world or his view of tragedy, which he said was his central interest?

BARR: I think I do. I may not understand it in exactly the way he does, but it's been a helpful corrective to me. As you know, I'm inclined to see life pretty much as comedy. He always says that about me. I think that there have been times in his life when my capacity to laugh has been actually an assistance to him, and certainly his power to see the tragic pattern in events has been of assistance to me. As a matter of fact, you know, I don't think comedy and tragedy get along very well unless they come to terms with each other, because life is both comic and tragic. And I don't think Scott has ever had the optimism that I said Southerners complained of in the Yankee. He never had that adolescent sort of boy scout optimism, but neither does he have the disillusionment of a defeated people. Yet it is in some sense the defeat of the human race that makes him talk about the embers of the world.

WOFFORD: Were his main lines clear to you at Oxford? Was the melancholia there? The interest in tragedy?

BARR: Yes, but I bridle a little at the word "melancholia," though I can't state the case against it.

95

WOFFORD: It's used against him.

BARR: Oh, I know, and very widely. I don't think I know why I bridle.

WOFFORD: He keeps that picture of melancholia above his desk, in his sight.

BARR: Yes. I would be willing to call it melancholia and let it go at that, if it were not that Scott has a robust faith in the things he has a faith in. He hasn't got faith in most of the things that most of my friends trust and have faith in, but he has a much deeper faith, I think, in the significance of the human experience than they have. So I'm tempted to say he can afford the luxury of melancholia. I think most of my friends would probably be led off to the bughouse if they indulged their melancholia because they haven't got much faith. He can contemplate the tragic without being debilitated by his contemplation of it, and I don't think they can. I think the typical optimist is optimistic because he fears failure and death so much that he's whistling through the graveyard. I never heard Scott whistle through one—never heard him whistle at all. I think I had a lot of this, and that's why he was painful to me when I first knew him.

And I think I still have some kind of queer faith in that baby, as distinguished from babyhood. He has faith in ideas beyond mine. I suppose you have to live with ideas more than I have in order to have his kind of faith in them. He really trusts the human intellect in a way almost nobody else I know intimately has trusted it. I think most of the people who've admired and even loved him have admired and loved him because they've detected this.

WOFFORD: You found this when you first collided?

BARR: Yes, but not very explicitly. I don't think I could have explained it to myself. It was just that his mind was deeply interesting.

WOFFORD: What were his views on Napoleon?

barr: Oh, God, I don't even know that I can remember. I think he probably was doing the thing that he's been doing in the last five years in relation to his concern over law. He was saying Napoleon was not just a tyrant or murderer but that he really had a problem of the human intellect, the unification of Europe—which Europe badly needed and certainly has paid hideous prices for not having achieved. I think Scott did a kind of ironical whitewash of Napoleon, which interested and amused me, and so I whitewashed him in my oral examination, and the tutor was grinning from ear to ear when he congratulated me and gave me honors.

WOFFORD: One way in which you and Scott parted company was on this question of the world you stayed in and acted in, in terms of political interest and responsibility, and which he denied for many years.

BARR: That's true.

WOFFORD: He didn't vote for a long time?

BARR: No, there were many years he didn't vote. I voted as soon as I could. Politics has always interested me very deeply—I'm very Southern on this, or Anglo-Saxon maybe. I'm a little ashamed of how deeply it interests me, because even just political maneuver, or low level politics kind of fascinates me. He's always been amused that I was fascinated by it. In the last few years, of course, in fact ever since World War II, he has a great deal more political interest, but it's very different from mine. Maneuver tends to bore him. We used to quarrel about Roosevelt when we were both living in Charlottesville. He thought Roosevelt was—

WOFFORD: Just a maneuverer?

BARR: He thought he was playing it pretty loose with the Constitution, striking it pretty hard. He admitted his maneuvers were for good causes, but he thought the bill would come in for that. He talked like the best kind of conservative Republican in his arguments, and I was saying, "Well this stuff has to be done." Except for the Supreme Court episode, which hit when we were in Chicago that year, Roosevelt very rarely displeased me. It seemed to me he saw the really important issues for this country and got a lot of them into business, and in order to do it he certainly did a lot of things that politicians do, but I was fascinated by him.

WOFFORD: How did Scott play the political game when he was in it, as chairman of the Chicago committee, or as a professor, or as dean?

BARR: He didn't. I don't think he really consented to "play politics" in any sense. His relationship with people around him was always a sort of a Socratic relation.

WOFFORD: What does a Socratic administrator do to an institution?

BARR: A lot of people would tell you he just raises hell with it. On the other hand somebody was telling me the other day that he'd been in Annapolis and ran into one of the faculty who had been there in our day, and this man was still stirred up by Buchanan—he said nothing like it had ever happened anywhere in the world. Yet I happen to know this faculty member was quite a problem and very much resented some of Scott's stuff when we were there. I'm sure he would have then said that Scott was destructive, that he'd build something and tear it down. Maybe now he wouldn't say it, looking back. It's funny, funny stuff to remember.

IV

METAPHORS

[February 18, 1967]
with
Roger Landrum and David Schickele

Law and Politics

WOFFORD: Roger Landrum, David Schikele and I just came back from that mountain above you.

BUCHANAN: San Marcos Pass.

WOFFORD: We saw a fire there, but the bigger fire was the sunset. Across the hills a monastery started ringing its bells, and I remembered your account long ago of how the bells of the monastery rang in modern civilization. And with it came your Homeric catalogue of monastery, kibbutz, corporation, the list of corporate ships that helped entice me to law school.

BUCHANAN: You misheard the first. I could never have said the monastery bell rang in civilization. You just made that up.

WOFFORD: No. Maybe it was originally from Mumford, the story of how the monastery bells signaled the beginning of organized work, including agriculture.

BUCHANAN: The rest I follow. It made you go to law school, and then what?

WOFFORD: I'm still going from one of those corporate ships to another. But how did you get to the kibbutz and the corporation? For the twenty years I've known you those have been very major ideas.

BUCHANAN: The list is from Frederick Maitland's *Introduction* to Gierke, one of his books on the corporation. It's a long wonderful list. I put it in *Essay on Politics*. But I'll tell you about the argument this morning at the Center just before you came. We were all talking about cities, and I was giving my notion of what the city ought to do about the corporate complex.

WOFFORD: What is that?

BUCHANAN: They're getting all mixed up. The profit corporation and the charitable corporation are combining in various ways; and the profit corporation is combining with the public corporation, the government in other words, making contracts of all sorts; and also the government is combining with the charitable corporation, the universities. They're all hooked in some awful tangle, and the municipal corporation is in the middle. It's one of the public corporations that suffers the most. If you could make some sense of the corporation law and get new kinds of charters for cities, you might have a city government again. History doesn't show that cities have ever had good governments, except possibly Athens and an Italian city-state like Florence. But now we have to have them.

WOFFORD: Where did you first come to the idea of the corporation?

BUCHANAN: In a very concrete way, a way that you may discover, sir. I discovered that a college is a corporation. When the Navy tried to take over our campus at Annapolis in order to expand in the second world war, I began reading law again; I began reading cases.

You know the Dartmouth College case? It's a great educational story.

WOFFORD: Is the making of contracts and corporations the heart of law as you see it?

BUCHANAN: I'm not sure about that. I'm more and more puzzled by law. I was saying to myself the other day: the one thing I don't know about law, the longer I study it, is what a law is—and what its real essence is. It's the most complicated business.

WOFFORD: Who is saying what to whom?

BUCHANAN: I was saying this to myself.

WOFFORD: No. I mean a question about a law is who is saying what to whom and with what sanction. Isn't a law something that has been said by somebody to somebody else?

BUCHANAN: That's not the great classical definition. Law is a rule of reason. Primarily it isn't a command, but a rule of reason. It's promulgated by an authority, according to St. Thomas, but for the common good—that is, a rule of reason promulgated by an authority for the common good.

WOFFORD: But you and Gandhi have done a twist on that and said this rule of reason becomes a question to everybody to whom it's directed.

BUCHANAN: A rule of reason might be a question. It can be stated in almost any mood. A rule of reason is just a general statement.

WOFFORD: Don't you say every rule of reason *is* a question, to a person with reason, with a conscience?

BUCHANAN: Yes. I'd want to say dialectically that any statement is also a question. This is following Buber and people like him. That is, there is a phase of any statement that is a question. You can put a question mark after anything. But this shouldn't be seen as *the* essence of the law; it's an aspect of it. The essence of it is the rule.

WOFFORD: Which is enforced.

BUCHANAN: That's not added in the big definition. I've had arguments about that here with those who are strong on the enforcement, the sanctions, the coercion. Austin stresses it: when a command is given, backed by a sanction, that's what he says a law is. That's the positivist school of law—not the great classical school. But these are all controversial questions. I've just got on my desk now *The Pure Theory of Law* by Kelson. I'm going to start and read some of these big works. I haven't ever read Austin.

WOFFORD: When did you start reading law?

BUCHANAN: In any continuous way it started with the Dartmouth College case when the Navy was attacking St. John's in World War II. I read Daniel Webster's plea and Marshall's opinion. Together they make a kind of treatise on corporation law, a kind of history of the corporation. That started me reading other cases in corporation law.

WOFFORD: Then you moved fast. Didn't you come back to St. John's in 1947 and say that you would re-do the curriculum and put law at the center?

BUCHANAN: Something like that. I left St. John's in '46 and came back to speak at Commencement. I said the college ought to have a subject matter as well as the liberal arts—a subject matter you could find in the great books if necessary but, whether you've got the great books or not, there ought to be a nameable and followable subject matter, a theme. And I thought law, in college, should be that. This came from an interest in politics more than law itself, although it was backed by the reading in law that I'd done at the time.

WOFFORD: You moved into politics quickly. By 1948 you were active in the Progressive Party campaign and in an encounter then you called me a fascist. I was opposing Henry Wallace and we were arguing about the role of Communism and Communists. You said the theory I was following was ultimately a fascist theory.

BUCHANAN: I'm sorry I did, because I don't really approve of using words that way.

WOFFORD: But it was unusual to find you in the midst of a political campaign, wasn't it?

BUCHANAN: It was the first time in my life, yes.

WOFFORD: Is it true you had never voted before?

BUCHANAN: That's true.

WOFFORD: Defend yourself.

BUCHANAN: I don't know I have much defense to make. I believed a teacher, having academic freedom and within the teaching function a good deal of influence, probably shouldn't be involved directly in politics. Academic freedom for me in those days was a sort of deal. If the state will leave me alone in my teaching, I'll leave it alone in what it does. I felt this very strongly, not because I'd had any trouble with it, but because I knew there would be trouble somewhere, sometime, and one had better be ready for it.

It was sometime during the St. John's experience that I completely shifted on all that, chiefly because of international politics. I thought it was everybody's duty to get into the business. I wasn't then persuaded very much to get into national politics. I didn't vote because I wasn't registered and I was lazy, I guess. It was not a very strong point with me—negligence, half of it.

I could say a great deal more. Take an election in California. Why do you vote? It's the damnedest feeling of impotence. It doesn't make any difference. Everything's playing house. It isn't just that it's too big and complicated to understand. It's that nobody who is in politics really means it—or so it appears. But I sort of conscientiously have voted ever since, for 20 years.

WOFFORD: How did you get to the Progressive Party? Out of nonpolitics into that strong a politics?

BUCHANAN: A peculiar set of incidents. The Navy coming to take us over, wounded me pretty badly. I didn't think *our* government would do such things. I began to feel things were getting out of hand, and probably this was due to the fact a lot of people weren't paying very much attention—the way I hadn't been. It was time we started to do something about it.

Just after the war, Joe Finley, an organizer for discussion groups of some sort, first for civilian youth, I think, came to Pittsfield where I was living, and interested the Mohills—Leon Mohill, a newspaper distributor, and his wife Sonia, had been in local politics a good deal and were sort of leftist in color. They got me in, and inside our discussion group we began talking about liberalism and what had happened to it, and finally the whole business of the Progressive Party came up. It wasn't called that then, you know, for it was a combination of several groups.

WOFFORD: The Political Action Committee of the CIO? CIO-PAC?

BUCHANAN: That's right, and some artists' and professionals' political groups. A fight began and ADA and the Progressive Party came out of it. You remember the split? The ADA would have nothing to do with Communists, and the Progressive Party people said anyone can join us; we're not concerned whether they're Communists or not. We belonged to that, and began working hard for it. The Mohills had a lot to do with pushing me. I think they thought I was kind of new and interested and perhaps could do good work. But anyway they pushed me and I was on the state committee and finally on the national platform committee.

About December of that year, '47, Henry Wallace announced he was going to run. I did things I'd never done before: rang doorbells and helped raise money, made speeches. Probably the most spectacular for me—

one time we went to the gates of the General Electric Company in Pittsfield, and I made a speech to the workers at noon as they came out. This was novel—I'd never even seen one of these before. I was introduced as one who would sympathize with labor because I was putting a roof on a garage out in the country. I don't think I made any impression that day.

How to Float Communism

WOFFORD: I heard you were equally unsuccessful when you urged the local group to spend the winter reading Marx.

BUCHANAN: This was after the campaign was all over. They wanted to go on, and I didn't want to just organize some more. I thought probably it would be better if we informed ourselves about some things, and I suggested we read Marx. It had a very interesting effect. We didn't make a point of detecting Communists in our midst, but we had vague notions about them and used to talk about it among ourselves—but this separated them out right away. They left. We lost all of our Communists because I proposed reading Marx.

WOFFORD: Why?

BUCHANAN: Against orders, they said later. They didn't say it then, they just silently left, but it was a very funny feeling.

WOFFORD: Like the church in the old days not wanting people to read the Bible?

BUCHANAN: Very much, I think. They thought it would confuse everybody. They had much simpler things to say. As a matter of fact, after we got this seminar going and did read Marx there were some older Marxians who joined us—some people from Hashomer

Hatzair in Israel, and a man who was a psychiatrist at the Riggs Clinic and his wife. And we had terrible quarrels. They said I was misleading them, that I was not an expert on Marx at all. I wasn't giving them the right line and they were up in arms about this. They were scholars of a sort and thought this was terrible, what I was doing.

WOFFORD: What was your theory then, on Marxism or Communists in American politics?

BUCHANAN: I've reshifted a lot—I learned a lot about the whole business. From some point when I was a young man I had assumed socialism was in the future—that it was the trend of events. It would happen by itself and I was on that side. I didn't join any party and didn't get much interested in it; but I think I took it for granted. And the Communists—as people, I knew quite a few of them, in college and graduate school and teaching. Some rather close friends were party members, and it's always interested me; we always talked about it. But I always found it very difficult to make any real applications of Marxian doctrine to American life. It didn't seem to me to fit anywhere. It had a very general application, but not strict. Socialism of the British variety is much more relevant to things here, I thought.

But I never thought Communists were very dangerous people. They didn't seem to me to be very effective. Some of them had pretty good minds and I liked to talk to them. I finally read all of Marx—all I could get hold of then—and even talked about it in philosophy classes a good deal, but it never really registered very heavily with me. Nor did the presence of Communists interest me much. I used to get exercised about civil liberties when they got pushed around. When the New Deal came along, I realized a good deal of it was sparked by Communists in the government, and this interested me—that there were people who really cared enough to do something about it.

WOFFORD: Rather than hoping or helping to make things all go to pot?

BUCHANAN: No. I meant the early Communists I knew were more or less parlor Communists. They didn't really work very hard, but there were people in Washington that seemed to be working very hard.

WOFFORD: Not to break or stop the machine, but to make it work? You're saying there were Communists in the government who were in fact advancing the New Deal, rather than being there in order to help break the whole thing?

BUCHANAN: I still don't think of Communists as people who want to break things. We can get into another argument on that point.

WOFFORD: The revolution?

BUCHANAN: Yes, they may want a revolution, but that isn't just breaking things up. They're not just naughty Communists who want to smash things.

WOFFORD: There certainly appears to be a wing of the Communist Party here, and in India which hopes to advance the revolution by seeking to make things worse.

BUCHANAN: Yes. But we are talking about revolutionary tactics, aren't we? It's a complicated story—whether Communists want to make things worse so they'll get better. Maybe so, but it's a side argument. No, I meant Communists were finding the government fellow-traveling with them, and were doing rather remarkable work. At the end of the Progressive Party when we began talking about it all some people who had been more sympathetic and more cooperative with the Communists than the rest of us made an interesting point. The Communists in this country, and the leftists in general, have had always a very special function, they

107

said. When things get bad they plunge in and do things—they spark movements of populism and reform—and get kicked around before they get through.

WOFFORD: Like the CIO. They helped organize that.

BUCHANAN: Yes, and then got kicked out. It seems their fate to do this over and over again.

WOFFORD: The civil rights movement?

BUCHANAN: Yes. And this gives a certain plausibility to Communist hunters—the baiters—who go around and say back of all these things are Communists. Well they are there. Very often they didn't start it at all, but they are there and sometimes they're the people who really make things go when other people haven't got enough energy and determination to do it.

WOFFORD: Why do you think this is so?

BUCHANAN: Because Communism has a certain kind of reality and integrity all its own. A lot of Communists are people who do things because they think they ought to be done, and they have the guts to do it.

WOFFORD: Communists have an ideology that shows them what to do. You came back from Israel saying a little girl asked you, "How can Americans live without an ideology?"

BUCHANAN: This was a pretty general question asked by Israeli kids in high school. They were very curious as to why American children didn't have an ideology. How did they live without an idea of the world? Yes, there's that in it. To put it in other terms, if you want to look at it as a philosophy or a reasoned position about something, Communism has more of that than most of American politics. In the old days, there was a kind of liberalism that had that, and there's still some of that left in the South.

WOFFORD: My recollection is that our first argument on this had to do with your case that it is necessary and important to help contain Communism and Marxism in its full form in American politics, and some people should try to do this.

BUCHANAN: Yes. I said the aim of the Progressive Party was to float Communism. Bring it into a party in which it wouldn't be the dominating effect, but would have a life. It didn't have any life. It was a shadowy thing that couldn't have any effect at all, and it ought to have some medium in American political life. The Progressive Party was offering that. Rex Tugwell always said, "Yes, but I'd say *swamp*." He thought the Progressive Party would swamp Communism.

WOFFORD: In the Soviet Union there's no party permitted—there's no way yet to float the democratic republican idea, and in the United States, which purports to be republican, to be an open society, it's almost impossible to surface the other major political idea in the world. The conditions for political dialectic are disappointing almost everywhere.

BUCHANAN: Yes. Dorothy Healy, who is the secretary for Southern California of the Communist Party, quite openly, came here about two years ago, pleading with us to have some real, steady contact with the Communists. Not necessarily to have one on our staff, but to have people come and talk to us. She said one reason is that you people ought to know more about Communism than you do. But she said secondly: "I'm pleading with you. We have no political life. We don't know what's going on." She said the youngsters now getting interested, as soon as they join her, are cut-off from the rest of society. They don't belong to anything, they don't get the news even in a straight way.

WOFFORD: What did you and your colleagues say?

BUCHANAN: A very simple thing; we said if you've got any good ones we'd like to have some. And she said, "There's Mr. Aptheker." And we said we don't believe he's very good—he's a bore.

Great Zionism and Little Zionism

WOFFORD: How did you get to the kibbutz?

BUCHANAN: That came immediately after the Progressive Party campaign. The Mohills had been thinking of going to Israel for some time. So as soon as the campaign was over, and partly because they were disappointed in what went on, they thought they would go to Israel to see if they wanted to move there with their three daughters. This was the fall of '49, and you may remember we were going from The Foundation for World Government to Stockholm for a meeting of the world government movement. So I went with them to Israel for two weeks while they did their scouting.

This was a wonderful two weeks. We did Israel from Dan to Beersheba, literally, and saw the kibbutzim, particularly. Leon and Sonia would be fighting about what they were seeing, always arguing like mad, and we were in on the conversation whenever we wanted to be. Listening to it was wonderful. We got more out of Israel than you'd get out of any tour by witnessing this. We didn't really get to the kibbutz on that trip. We saw them at a distance and went in some where we were strangers. We got the feel of it. They decided before the two weeks were up they were going to go there, and we more or less agreed that when they had been there, they would see we got there again in some way. So in another two years we were back for six months.

WOFFORD: On what assignments?

BUCHANAN: Well, a friend of theirs was in the Federation of Kibbutzim called Kibbutz Artzi Hashomer Hatzair.

WOFFORD: What does that stand for?

BUCHANAN: The Federation of Land Settlements of the Young Watchmen. Each of these words has a very special meaning. "Kibbutz" means the ingathering of the exiles; it's also in Russian a federation. And "Artzi" is derived from the old Hebrew word "erets" which means the land of Israel, a very special word for Jews. "Hashomer" is the watchman, the name for one of the youth movement organizations that formed this organization. And "Hatzair" is "young." This was originally part of the youth movement, a kind of boy scout movement. This was a group of youngsters who trained as pioneers, and when Israel opened after the First World War, they went and started kibbutzim. This had gone on steadily during the mandate until, when we went there, there were about 65 kibbutzim.

WOFFORD: Long long ago I remember sitting on the lawn at St. John's hearing you talk under the great tree—your commencement address in 1952. You said the three Hebrew words—*diaspora, aliya,* and *kibbutz*—represented the three motions of this world. What about those other two words?

BUCHANAN: *Diaspora* of course is the dispersal, that is the exile, the 2,000-year wandering of the Jews—being away from home, in some sense still scattering; not in community. *Aliya* is "going up," which means going up to Jerusalem really, a coming back. And *kibbutz* is the ingathering. This is the Zionist movement, of course.

WOFFORD: Are these the motions of the world?

BUCHANAN: At the end of that speech I was saying I felt all of us were in the diaspora, and I wished we might have some way of going up and ingathering—a resettlement, if you want to use Doxiadis' word. These were movements I thought were going on in the world. Or perhaps to go back to Smuts: after the first world war he said people are on the march—they've struck their tents and are on the march—and they're looking for resettlement of some kind. This has been going on for two generations.

WOFFORD: What did you see in Israel during your six months in 1951?

BUCHANAN: What it really means to be a wandering Jew, and therefore, perhaps a wandering Gentile. What it takes to go up, and form a community.

WOFFORD: Your report was called *The Next Generation of Hashomer Hatzair*. What was your diagnosis?

BUCHANAN: I told them at the end of this report that they had lost some of the great Zionism they had started with. I knew the reasons for it and was sympathetic but I made the distinction between great Zionism and little Zionism. Great Zionism is the generalization of the thing, the view that if they can do this, to use a Biblical phrase again, light will break forth from Zion for the rest of the world, and Israel can be in some sense a school of the world. That is what their great leaders had always been dedicated to, but they, because of the very hard life, had begun to feel little and small and when they talk about Zionism it was really a sort of pathetic plea that they be allowed to survive, barely. This was too bad. They ought to see if they couldn't somehow remount the whole project in the next generation. Their youngsters would, I thought, but they should get help for this.

WOFFORD: What was your prescription?

BUCHANAN: I had four or five things. It seemed to me they needed to take more account of their corporate structure; they needed to be concerned more about their health than they were, in a better way; and two or three things like that which I had no business telling them. I was there to talk about education. On that I said they ought to start a university of the kibbutzim, rather than just send their children to the Hebrew University.

WOFFORD: Why?

BUCHANAN: They were refusing to send their children to the university, because they came back no longer responsible members of the kibbutz. They began to be careerists. They began to get education so they could go off and have a high life of some kind or other. And this, for a kibbutznik, was kind of treason to the community. So they wanted to have their own thirteenth year in the kibbutz school. And I said what you need is a university.

WOFFORD: You thought they could form one that wouldn't have the same careerist emphasis that all universities I know of have in the world today?

BUCHANAN: I thought then that they could. I proposed they set this up on the shore, in an old crusaders' castle. Wonderful old buildings were there which they could use. It could become a world university. Later I had a better idea, to start a university again on Mt. Scopus. There was still an Israeli enclave where Hebrew University had been. A world university there, combining a technical school like MIT and a full university like Harvard, under some world auspices, such as the UN or some world corporation you might set up, could be their salvation, and do a great thing for the world.

WOFFORD: It might have taken the children away from the kibbutz forever. It might have sent them to Africa and India and Latin America to organize kibbutzim or other new ventures.

BUCHANAN: As they are already beginning to do now. They sent Peace Corps people, their kind of *Schlichim*—messengers—to other places in the world—Africa, particularly and some to Burma.

WOFFORD: *Garin*—new pioneers going out.

BUCHANAN: Yes, *Garin*.

WOFFORD: Why did you propose that the Foundation for World Government send a group of us over in the summer of 1950?

BUCHANAN: I thought this would give a tempting experience and a little training for people who might be willing to go and work in development projects in various parts of the world, in something like a kibbutz arrangement. I didn't mean this as literally as you took it later, that they should go in for kibbutz organizations in a literal style, but I thought they might go in pairs, to spend the rest of their lives doing this—more in the fashion of my old yen to get to India.

Cultivate Your Neurosis

WOFFORD: In planning our new college at Old Westbury, somebody once finally said, "What we really want is to produce people like us, or people who will do the things we thought we ought to do." And we all found ourselves doing that.

BUCHANAN: That's right. I used to have a dream, when Woodrow Wilson was trying to get a League of Nations going, of being his assistant—his man Friday or something. I saw this leading to a corps of world citizens who would give up their nationality, give up their citizenship, and spend their lives working for the League of Nations.

WOFFORD: Did Gary Davis revive that dream when he declared himself a world citizen?

BUCHANAN: I recalled it to him, yes. A very peculiar, very vivid dream. I can still remember it. There was a long table, with green felt on it, under those funny old lights with conical shades that hang down from overhead. Wilson was sitting at one end of the table and I was sitting at the other. The rest of the meeting had gone and we were talking. Along with it went another funny thing—white uniforms for some reason. This gets to be very bad; I'm sure that Freud could make a great story of it. Very funny stuff.

WOFFORD: What other dreams do you have?

BUCHANAN: I have another kind of dream I shouldn't tell, I suppose, at all. A terrible dream. There are many variations on it. The first time I remember having this kind of dream was just after college. I had a dream I was playing a pipe organ and didn't know how to play, and it was before a big audience. And I kept on playing and didn't know how. Terrific fear—horror. Since then I've had variations on this: a motorman on a trolley car and the tracks disappear. I'm sure this is a very deep dream.

WOFFORD: Have you ever worked on any dreams?

BUCHANAN: No.

WOFFORD: Have you ever thought of psychoanalysis?

BUCHANAN: Yes. I thought of doing that very seriously when I was working on the philosophy of medicine.

WOFFORD: I have a good friend who just finished and said it was his Ph.D. It was far more educational than any of the academic degrees he'd ever had.

BUCHANAN: He probably had an easy case. It often isn't, you know. When there's really deep trouble, it often doesn't come off and then it's awful. It's a diseducation. It's what I'm a little afraid of with all this group therapy that's going on.

WOFFORD: It might cause deep trouble for some of the people who go into it?

BUCHANAN: There is this possibility, I think. Take the ordinary person—a troubled student, if you like—put him in this situation and it's very intense. No punches are pulled and they go at it with great verve. This sort of frightens me. They say it's wonderful—they say it straightens things out for them like mad.

WOFFORD: The chief psychiatrist of the Peace Corps is very resistant to all the T-groups, encounter groups, and group therapy for this reason; he thinks a great many people, if not most people, generally need their defenses. They need manners; as in *A Man for All Seasons,* they need the trees there to hide behind.

BUCHANAN: Do you want a world all flattened out for you? You want people with prejudices and senses of humors and roles to play and so on—that's what human life is. You don't want it rolled out so everyone loves everybody else and understands themselves completely.

WOFFORD: Where does Freud come out on this?

BUCHANAN: I think Freud would be kind of horrified. Freud had a high sense, it seems to me, of form and style and skill—discipline. He knew how deep this went. Most psychoanalysts in this country, at least at present, don't seem to me to take psychoanalysis very seriously. Freud did. You know the issues between Marcuse and the rest of the sociologists and the psychiatrists? Marcuse is saying Freud was a real revolutionary. But no American psychoanalyst is. They're all adjusting. That isn't what psychoanalysis is talking about at all.

WOFFORD: How is Freud a revolutionary?

BUCHANAN: He knew the psyche doesn't necessarily straighten itself out. He was a pessimist about this. He thought you might be able to discover, to know, but you might in the end not want to do much about it. It would be revolutionary in the sense that if you do do anything about it, you know you're going to change society and a whole lot of things as well. His pessimism about society would be the corollary of this.

WOFFORD: Would you say a little bit more about dis-education or levelling?

BUCHANAN: Karen Horney I think is the one who has this formula stronger than most others. The aim of such psychoanalysis would be to adjust yourself to your environment, the human environment as well as others, but Freud is saying, it seems to me: Not to this society. Don't try to adjust yourself to this one. This is a bad society. In order to be yourself, genuinely—I don't know whether you'd say to be happy—but in order to be yourself, integrated in some way and have insight, it may mean you have to be a revolutionary and try to take over the society. And if you make education the way by which you assimilate or conform yourself to society you may be doing a great deal of damage to yourself. That's what American psychoanalysis very often is. It's a weak form of Freud.

WOFFORD: I remember you once prescribed, "Cultivate your Neurosis."

BUCHANAN: People who are really creative and happy in some genuine way are often those who have neuroses and follow them.

WOFFORD: Don't try to dispose of your dreams but do something about them?

BUCHANAN: Cultivate them. That is, work them out.

WOFFORD: How does your Israel dream hold up? What did you mean at the end of your kibbutz report when you said that you came back from that expedition to Syracuse like Plato—in chains.

BUCHANAN: It was a bad ending. I had had a rather tough time in Israel—and they had had a rather tough time with me. I added just a little slap, that's all. I probably shouldn't have said it at all. You know, Plato gets sent home from Syracuse by the man he had been trying to teach, and I just said I sent myself home before you sent me. It didn't come off. I had intended it to be light and witty.

WOFFORD: You once led a seminar in the Riggs Clinic for mentally ill people?

BUCHANAN: It was while I was living in Richmond, Massachusetts—in the late 40's I guess. Joan Erikson, Erik Erickson's wife, was then in charge of the occupational therapy and other things they were doing, like drama, and she thought it would be a good idea if I led a great books seminar. It turned out to be very, very good, one of the best seminars I've ever had. Schizophrenia is ideal for a good seminar. If you want to put on a real show, get some schizophrenics together and have them do this with you.

It was agreed I shouldn't try to make this a therapeutic thing at all. Just do it as you would with normal people. But I got to know a good deal about them and they used to come over and see me, ten miles away where I lived. One night we had been reading and discussing Antony and Cleopatra. One of the girls, one of the best people in the seminar, had been a classics graduate student at Bryn Mawr and had been very much interested in most of the books we had read. I was a little curious as to where she was but I didn't notice anything very special. It had been a terribly good discussion and at the end I said, "We've been discussing this as though it were a tragedy, but suppose Shakespeare really wrote this as a comedy?" And she blew her top and next day tried to commit suicide. It turned out Cleopatra was her idol and this had disturbed her terribly. I shouldn't have been disturbed by this particularly because, you know, patients do this without such a cause, too, but it disturbed me. I went to Joan Erikson and said I think you'd better call this off. I think I want to know more about what I'm up to if I do it or I don't want to do it at all.

WOFFORD: Did she let you call it off?

BUCHANAN: Yes.

WOFFORD: You wouldn't call off good powerful intensive seminars in a college for that reason, would you?

BUCHANAN: No. I was telling a psychiatrist about this just last week, and he said, "You shouldn't have done that. You weren't doing anything dangerous at all. Those patients go through these things; you weren't responsible for it." And I said, "Yes, but I just had a feeling I ought to know more about them if I was having that much effect."

WOFFORD: Do you have the feeling sometimes you're doing something dangerous in a powerful seminar? Is the reverse of the Riggs story true: can really good seminars produce schizophrenia?

BUCHANAN: There was a time at St. John's when we began turning up schizophrenics rather frequently. One year we must have had half a dozen, and perhaps some we didn't recognize. I knew the Phipps Clinic pretty well so I used to go with them very often when they needed help and introduce them to the doctor. On one occasion I stayed afterwards and said to the doctor, "Some of our enemies have been telling us we're going to turn out this sort of thing just because of what we're doing, the great books and all this heavy intellectual work." He said, "The other colleges are worse—you may get them a little earlier; you may recognize them a little quicker, that's all." I think that's true. I don't think there's any connection really, except in a good seminar with an intelligent teacher, a good teacher, you do know what's going on, and you catch this kind of thing along with a lot more.

People connected with sensitivity training, group therapy and all this kind of thing tell us that this would be something new—that most teachers don't know this about their students. I find this false and appalling because good teachers have always known this kind of thing. They don't pay special attention to it—that isn't what a teacher should do. If you pay special attention to it that means something has really broken down and you're no longer a teacher. All this psychopathology or emotion or whatever else you call the non-rational stuff, you know in a good seminar much better than you would if you stepped back from it and tried to diagnose it. You might not call it any of the names—that wouldn't be your way of dealing with it—but you would know people were having difficulties.

WOFFORD: A St. John's student said to me that one of the dangers in the intense experience that went on there is that if you took seriously the idea of following the question where it leads, or the idea of entertaining every question, you would ultimately entertain the ultimate question, suicide.

BUCHANAN: Is that the ultimate question? I didn't think it was.

WOFFORD: It's not for me.

BUCHANAN: I can see how in a certain mood you'd think so. But I should think that was a good question to think about once in a while.

DAVID SCHICKELE: I have a more cheerful question, possibly, if I may intervene. How does this Socratic approach help you? How do you use it in daily life when you're unhappy in love or had an argument with your girl friend or your son? Does it spill over to questions that affect the things you do everyday?

BUCHANAN: I don't really know. I could make a guess but I can't answer directly. I'd guess this Socratic temper in general would produce a certain kind of sense of humor about all these things—sort of a detached one. I don't mean alienation—no concern—but a certain distance and the sense of humor to deal with it. Wouldn't it?

SCHICKELE: It seems so often when people talk about the Socratic question and following it where it leads, it is in an inner realm that has little relation to the world I know. Earlier we were talking about law and what is a law, and you say a law should be a question, a dialogue, so you see people being thrown in jail every day in San Francisco for doing things I think they have every right to do. It's all very nice to

120

talk about—you know, let's sit down and this law is a question—but that kind of talk about law is too removed from my immediate concerns about the problems of the law in this country. We are concerned not only with social organization and with the organization of thought, but also with the solving of personal problems. I am asking whether the whole Socratic way helps you not only crawl out of the cave in terms of your understanding of the social order around you, but also helps you crawl out of your own personal cave in one way or another in your relationship with other people.

BUCHANAN: I doubt very much if the Socratic thing should ever be given the literal psychoanalytic meaning, that is, that you know your own soul. I doubt if that is the real meaning of the Delphic Oracle and Socrates when he says, "Know thyself." It's a much broader thing. You seek to know the world and who you are in it. You don't know something deep about your own self and how to maneuver and so forth. I don't believe it does that.

WOFFORD: David, aren't the people you say are in jail there because they did question the law and treat it as a question and answered that they didn't think the law was just.

SCHICKELE: But that's no way to run an argument, by throwing people into jail. It's a dirty trick in the middle of the argument.

BUCHANAN: If you want to take it on a very serious level, this is part of the argument, isn't it?

SCHICKELE: I want my reward on earth.

BUCHANAN: I think if you are going to be a conscientious objector, you had better expect to go to jail. It's a part of the argument in that sense, and should be—you should want it to be. I know how it feels to be one and not go to jail. There is a curious irresponsibility about that.

The Mystical Body and Other Corporations

WOFFORD: In your first book, *Possibility*, you said genius consists in yielding to the temptation of metaphor and mythology.

BUCHANAN: I was quoting Aristotle.

WOFFORD: Could you state what your master metaphors are? Israel? The kibbutz?

BUCHANAN: You see, from my point of view, if you do the liberal arts you do something similar to what we're doing with the question about law. A law is a question. This is a transformation in a dialectical fashion. You shift it out of its original framework and put it into another. What does it mean here? Anything can be a metaphor in this same way. The most literal statements you make can be a metaphor. We're here in this room. It's very easy to make this mean we're here in the world. This is the nature of language. It has a metaphorical nerve or force in it that spontaneously does this in your mind. So anything that can be said is a metaphor, and you should be able to do this always, without disturbing yourself too much. A lot of people get terribly upset and angry when they realize this. And that is a good first reaction to it, I guess, but you learn later this is something you can do always. You know one man's metaphor is another person's literal statement, and vice versa, in the ordinary way you deal with life. But you ought to be able to see both ways. So I don't think I have any favorite metaphor.

WOFFORD: Recurring ones: Big ones?

BUCHANAN: I suppose, yes. My largest categories—philosophical categories—I guess are comedy and tragedy. I suppose they're metaphors in a way, favorite ones. At least I can take them that way, and I realize they are in some way ultimate figures of speech—and therefore not identical with reality; therefore not literal, but reflective.

WOFFORD: Is the corporation in that sense a metaphor?

BUCHANAN: Yes. Even lawyers say this.

WOFFORD: From the mystical body of Christ?

BUCHANAN: Corporations are called fictions—fictive persons, and of course the great one is the mystical body of Christ. That's the king term in the whole corporate structure. No one would run the corporation—the meaning of it—any higher than that.

WOFFORD: My skeptical wife always pushes me very hard on that one, asking me to explain what I mean by the mystical body, and I don't do very well.

BUCHANAN: The mystical body of Christ? It's a tough one. You know the church hasn't done very well by it. The postponement in the Ecumenical Council was about this more than any other thing. It hasn't yet finished its job, not by any means, but it's started on it. This is literally the case. In 1870 there were two articles on the agenda of Vatican I—probably more, but two critical ones. One was the infallibility of the Pope, and this was discussed, settled, and accepted for the first time. But along with it and balancing it was the mystical body of Christ, that is, the nature of the Church. The Pope was to be infallible but the Church was the body over which he was ruling. The City of Rome was under siege and they adjourned the meeting as the issue came to a crisis. They never had another Vatican Council until this one, and it has left the Church lopsided ever since. I mean the infallibility of the Pope has been a harsh doctrine, a juridical doctrine, without any of the political complex that should go with it. That's what this whole new doctrine of the collegiality of the cardinals and bishops and so on is trying to supply—a thing that should have been done in 1870.

WOFFORD: And what is the kingpin doctrine?

BUCHANAN: The mystical body is the nature of the Church. It has at least three meanings, and they are hard to put together. One is the Eucharist itself, another is the resurrected Christ, and then there's the Church. Two of these are pretty closely associated. The Eucharist is a kind of seal you put upon the Church, the whole Church. When you eat Christ's body at the Eucharist, you are becoming a part of the substance of the body of Christ in this mystical sense. And that's what the Church is—you belong to the body of Christ.

WOFFORD: After the mystical body of Christ there isn't anywhere to go but down, but one place we might rest would be on your world university, on Mt. Scopus—that's still fairly high. Are you suggesting that anything less than trying to be a world university today is an inadequate educational venture?

BUCHANAN: You're thinking of your enterprise now?

WOFFORD: Yes.

BUCHANAN: I suppose if there should be a world university in the literal sense, separate from any country, all by itself, it should be an exemplary model for others.

WOFFORD: Since there is no one world university, shouldn't any new university seek to become a model?

BUCHANAN: Yes. In the old days, before I knew law, I used to think that was what the word and idea "university" meant. You know, the universe. It doesn't mean that, as you know.

WOFFORD: Colleges were nations.

BUCHANAN: Yes, but *universitas* is the technical Latin name for a corporation, any corporation. A university literally does mean a certain kind of corporation, but it doesn't mean the universe.

SCHICKELE: I have one question. We've been talking all day about education and about the Socratic process and I sense a sort of sad recognition of some unknowables. I'd just like to ask what you think is unknowable.

BUCHANAN: I have the beginnings of a rather elaborate theory about that. I've never really worked it out. It begins with certain kinds of distinctions about unknowables. There may be something that is absolutely unknowable. I don't know whether there is or not—something itself intrinsically not knowable. It doesn't come into human knowledge or any other knowledge. But then in relation to the human intellect, there are a whole string of things that are unknowable. The future is one of them, and there's the other very simple one, that if I know this—that is whatever you've got before you— it'll be at the cost of not knowing something else. I choose to know this. My mind is finite, in other words, and I have to know this, and if I know this, I can't know that. And there's a progressive notion here, passing from one of these to another. So there are lots of kinds of unknowables. Whether there is an ultimate unknowable, I don't know. You know, orthodox Catholic theology says God is something of that. He's ultimately unknowable in himself. There's a funny paradoxical notion in the middle of this because he is in one sense the most knowable thing there is: He gives intelligibility to everything else, but, for that very reason, is not himself knowable. Is that what you were asking about, though? Were you thinking again about the irrational?

Psychoanalysis, Narcissism, and Group Therapy

SCHICKELE: I was not searching for any particular answer. I was wondering if you were going to mention something about irrationality. I think what put the scene in my mind was when I was asking about Socratic methods in terms of personal knowledge. You seemed to shy away from that idea, and I don't know whether you were pushing that knowledge into the realm of psychiatric methods as opposed to Socratic methods or whether you think there is something basically unknowable about the way people are put together and the way they operate.

BUCHANAN: There are a lot of funny quirks around that question. I know when I was digging up the liberal arts, I was also at the same time interested in Mary Boole, who was George Boole's wife. She was involved in psychology and discovered for herself the unconscious before Freud published his stuff. Going through that with her I started asking a question that I understand is interesting to almost any psychiatrist: Why can't the individual psychoanalyze himself? There's a funny answer to it: One man has—Freud—and in doing it invented psychoanalysis. He had the help of a funny friend, who wasn't a psychoanalyst, and through him analyzed himself. This is still a question I think of, why if a man were a good liberal artist, if he could think abstractly and knew all these metaphorical and reflective things with symbols and ideas, why shouldn't he be able to straighten himself out? I've never gotten any good answer.

SCHICKELE: Let me phrase the question another way. In the definition of even knowledge, anything that is knowable has to be graspable by our reason. There's something that has no reason or has no form, unknowable. Do you have any ideas about the nature of chaos? What it is or whether it exists or what relation it has to all this we've been talking about?

BUCHANAN: I don't believe I have. Here again you can do some tricks with words because if there's anything at all that I don't understand it is chaos—that's a working meaning of chaos. But whether there is any intrinsic and *per se chaos*, I don't know. I should think not. Everything that's real is rational. You're in a puzzle right away. Is chaos real? If it is, it's rational. There's an awful lot of chaos in our experience, because we don't understand so much, and the more you do understand the more extensive and deeper the chaos is. You're aware of this as you expand your own experience. These are awfully hard questions to handle without a very thoroughgoing dialectical treatment which I've never worked out.

WOFFORD: Up on the mountain earlier David hit me for a line in an article critical of the mere personal exploration of psyches. I was saying that the real identity crisis is the identity of the world. He said, "What do you mean by *mere* personal exploration of psyche?" One of the good ideas coming out of the under-30 generation, he believes, is the idea that in a large proportion of life people should be meeting each other and listening to each other and trying to understand each other and helping each other to understand, like Freud and his friend were doing. He sees it as something that may be very important and promising, which ought to be somehow encouraged in the structure of our life and certainly in the structure of a college. We have to admit this is the part of life we don't provide for in our educational system, or our system of work, and it is one of the things a lot of the under-30 generation are seeking.

BUCHANAN: After a certain point I am completely unable to be sympathetic with the younger generation when it wants to do this. Up to a certain point I can—first I can concretely say, yes, that should be straightened out; then you push me a little farther and abstractly I can—but after a certain point I don't believe there's anything in it. It's a blind alley. You can call it various names: self-cultivation, or self-indulgence, or narcissism. There always are occasions when this is important but when it becomes general as it is now, and so habitually in regular cultivation, I lose sympathy and don't know how to judge it any more.

SCHICKELE: Why must you call it narcissism? The best thought of our best thinkers and our best social organizers and our best philosophers throughout the ages have not really helped much in terms of human happiness. It seems to me one of the reasons for this is we don't know what we are. Why are you so afraid of it?

BUCHANAN: I don't think I'm afraid of it. Maybe I'm blinding myself to it, but I just don't think it turns up anything. It's uninteresting to me. This is like the discussion of self-psychoanalysis. Why can't you do that? I'm not quite sure I know why, but I'm pretty sure there's some reason. I don't believe a human being is going to be able to do that. Then when you do it without skill to each other, I think this is perhaps going to be dangerous—to do some real damage. It doesn't frighten me particularly, but I think if it isn't done skillfully it's like bad doctors who can do a lot of damage.

SCHICKELE: I have to really disagree with you on that.

BUCHANAN: I imagine so, and there may be a deep reason, important heavy reasons why *you* should think this was very important right now. I'm not seeing just what that is.

SCHICKELE: I think partly it's a matter of personal interests. Some people are interested in music and other people aren't interested in it. I find people and who they are and the way they behave and what they think and feel more interesting than I find a lot of purely intellectual problems, and I'm beginning to think maybe in terms of any real progress in human happiness this is something that should be pursued more. You say it may be dangerous, but I feel like Bob Dylan says in the song, "When you ain't got nothing you ain't got nothing to lose"—things are bad enough for most people in many ways so that you aren't really running much of a danger. Any kind of education really is dangerous.

BUCHANAN: Are people that unhappy at present?

SCHICKELE: I think they are. I see a lot of unhappiness.

BUCHANAN: I agree with you but are they *that* unhappy. That is, that nothing could be worse?

SCHICKELE: I just don't in the first place share your feeling that it's dangerous and even if it does have its dangers, there's almost nothing worthwhile undertaking to try to learn that isn't dangerous in some way.

BUCHANAN: Sure, the world is dangerous, but I hate medical malpractice. Perhaps there could be better psychiatry than we've got, but I don't believe we're going to get that by this amateur stuff.

SCHICKELE: I'm not speaking specifically of psychiatry or of amateur self-psychoanalysis, I just mean people talking simply to each other about the things they feel in the way that society does not usually give them a chance to and that even in close personal relationships people don't really do. We hide so much of ourselves, so much of our lives, for so many reasons, in a way I don't think is necessarily beneficial, although obviously it makes things run smoother at the time.

BUCHANAN: Don't you want a little more fun?

SCHICKELE: Oh, but that's fun. It depends on what you're interested in, you know. You attacked Harris today for suggesting—although I don't think he really was—that book learning is not exciting. Obviously it is, but in the same vein, finding out about your friends can be exciting.

BUCHANAN: Yes.

WOFFORD: You're sounding sympathetic.

BUCHANAN: Oh, I am with this. I'm curious about other people. I like to gossip, too—but you don't like this way of talking about it, do you?

SCHICKELE: That is perhaps your comic sensibility.

BUCHANAN: Yes. It seems to me this is a dramatic curiosity we have about each other which I like to have satisfied, but I think you've got some more serious business in mind.

SCHICKELE: It's very hard to talk about. But there are so many things society at large frowns upon in people and refuses to recognize in people, and people even in their friend relationships and love relationships refuse to accept and recognize and deal with. By refusing to talk about these things—and I don't mean a dramatic self-confessional sort of thing—I think we deny so much of the reality around us. Some of the things in us may be pretty terrible and anti-social and most of us get along by just ignoring them. But I think there's something essentially stunting about this.

ROGER LANDRUM: I was very disturbed this morning by how casually so many of the Center people were calling a lot of other people uncivilized. There was a whole lack of both empathy and experience as to vast populations. I don't know very much about Athens but I understand this was characteristic of the citizens of Athens, too.

BUCHANAN: You mean calling others barbarians?

LANDRUM: Yes. Maybe that was because they didn't know themselves in a certain way well enough or they knew themselves too rationally. A lot of this really gets down to the fundamental racism between black people of African cultural derivation and white people of European derivation.

BUCHANAN: There's a big shift that you are talking about. I don't think it's that people are blind and insensitive, in a sort of flat way, but they're blind in the sense of something you see, they haven't seen recently or perhaps ever. Now this of course is something we ought to pay attention to. But you can be mistaken, too, and

I don't believe you learn about these things by paying direct attention to them. It's a little like the old stuff you can say about happiness: you can't get it by wanting it—you can't go after happiness and get it. I don't believe you can get this kind of knowledge by curiosity. It comes indirectly. I think I'd know more about you if we'd go out to do something together than if I'd say, "What do you like to do?"

SCHICKELE: You would probably learn twice as much by doing both.

BUCHANAN: What makes you think that? I don't agree.

WOFFORD: Why do you for the first time favor learning by doing instead of learning by thinking and talking and dialogue?

BUCHANAN: What we are doing here is talking about something—about something else, not about us. I'll learn more about you by talking about something else.

SCHICKELE: So little of me. Obviously in a certain sense people reveal their whole selves in the tiniest things they do, yet in another sense most of our social actions, involve only a small percentage not only of our consciousness, but of the things we are.

BUCHANAN: No, I think we understand each other pretty well without a lot of machinery around. We wouldn't be able to communicate if we didn't. Words alone can't do what you and I are doing right now. They couldn't possibly do it. It's a very complex sensibility we're playing with. Now I can turn around and look at some gesture you make, or call attention to various things that go into this, but I think I lose a good deal when I do. My eye isn't on the ball. I'm being curious in a silly way. I think that's what a lot of personal conversation is—not necessarily, though.

LANDRUM: I don't know if I fully understand the nature of your reluctance.

BUCHANAN: I think a Shakespeare play shows more

human stuff than any amount of my conversation would give anybody. True?

SCHICKELE: Yes. The realm of art is something different, although I think as art declines, as I think it is in a certain way, it's partly because certain life forces are coming up and art is no longer needed perhaps as much as it was—or something like that.

BUCHANAN: Oh, dear! We are talking about something rather difficult to talk about. You have to work at this very long and hard to be able to get to it. And you're not going to get very much by turning around and saying, "What are your funny prejudices?"

SCHICKELE: I really think you do get far that way.

BUCHANAN: Well I don't. Sociological epistemology! You know it's a big doctrine at present. Instead of listening to what a person's saying, you find out who he is, but you never come back to what he's saying, and so people don't say anything any more. The only thing that's interesting is people. That may be where we are; I'm a little afraid it is.

LANDRUM: There's something in between the T group and a St. John's seminar.

BUCHANAN: There are lots of varieties of these things. We don't have my kind of seminar here at all. We have a Hutchins seminar, which is a very funny cross-questioning thing. He makes lists of people that are going to talk, and they wait for their turn. You get a funny conversation this way. I'm exaggerating slightly because he sometimes will stop and say, "Do you want to talk on the same point we're talking here? I think there's more in this than we've got out—do you want to interrupt?" He does that once in a while.

WOFFORD: And your operating principle?

BUCHANAN: Follow the question. Pay attention to what's being said, not to the people—and you understand people very much better if you do this. To turn around and pay attention to the people is to lose what's being said. You make a choice when you do it.

SCHICKELE: You can't separate them.

BUCHANAN: I know. When you do one, you get something of the other, of course. I'm saying on the whole if you pay attention to what's being said you have a deeper insight.

SCHICKELE: You arrived at that empirically—out of your own experience?

BUCHANAN: Yes. This is an old philosophical question, so I've thought about it, too. It isn't just experience. There is a reflective knowledge that goes along with ordinary direct knowledge. You know what you're doing all the time. I'm not only thinking, I'm knowing I'm thinking when I'm thinking. And when I'm feeling, I know I'm feeling. You know this all the time.

LANDRUM: You do?

BUCHANAN: Sure. Don't you?

SCHICKELE: No.

BUCHANAN: You can't help it. It's spontaneous. Reason has this reflective power. It's the grandest power. That's a doctrinal point, I suppose. When you think this isn't so, reason or the intellect is dull—dull as hell—and it finally disappears.

WOFFORD: That's what's happened in academia.

BUCHANAN: Yes. That's what I think has happened. People don't think reason does this any more—so now we've got to do it the way you're suggesting, we've got to make a business of paying attention to our emotions. But do it in a highly integrated way, putting the emotions into your real rational life. Something has happened here to make this necessary, and this interests me very much. I'm more than respecting what you're saying. What happened that has broken it so badly?

WOFFORD: That's the question hanging over us—or as they say, we're hung up on this.

133

BUCHANAN: Yes. Let's turn ourselves on.

WOFFORD: Well shall we turn it off now?

SCHICKELE: I'm sorry, I'm afraid Roger and I have spoiled the purity of this dialogue.

BUCHANAN: No.

WOFFORD: But the people who come into the symposium at the end are supposed to come in drunk.

BUCHANAN: It's very funny to be making this argument after you've listened to me for a couple of hours talk about myself.

WOFFORD: The opposite also happens. You find some of the prophets of the personal exploration of psyche—of the realms that reason can't touch and of the non-verbal ways of knowing—the most reasonable, the most articulate and the most verbal.

V

THE GREAT LOVER
[February 19, 1967]
with
*Jacqueline Grennan, Roger Landrum and
David Schickele*

Ladders of Love

WOFFORD: "The Great Lover" by Rupert Brooke. That's the first poetry I've seen you deliver. It's at the end of your Ph.D. thesis, *Possibility*. What did Harvard's Philosophy Department think about a poem as the climax of a Ph.D. thesis?

BUCHANAN: They didn't like it and their way of expressing this was to say they didn't understand it. But when I went to the examination, there was Whitehead, and he sort of took over the examination. I'd never met him. He asked me rather searching questions in a most whimsical and gentle way. He was a wonderful person—a light high voice and rosy cheeks—gentle, imaginative, humorous. Lo and behold after an hour or so they told me that I'd passed. Then Whitehead invited me to his house and when I got there that evening he said, "You know, these people in the department told me that they didn't understand your thesis, and you know what my answer to them was? So much the worse for them."

WOFFORD: Did they take on the poem at all?

BUCHANAN: No, they didn't ask me about that. That was some sort of a little play I had to indulge in at the end and it was all right.

WOFFORD: Was that all it was?

BUCHANAN: The poem has a point, hasn't it?

WOFFORD: Here's what you said: "Imagine Aristotle the Greek observing actuality and let Rupert Brooke, who is more Greek than modern, speak for him:

THE GREAT LOVER

I have been so great a lover: filled my days
So proudly with the splendour of Love's praise,
The pain, the calm, and the astonishment,
Desire illimitable, and still content,
And all dear names men use, to cheat despair,
For the perplexed and viewless streams that bear
Our hearts at random down the dark of life.
Now, ere the unthinking silence on that strife
Steals down, I would cheat drowsy Death so far,
My night shall be remembered for a star
That outshone all the suns of all men's days.
Shall I not crown them with immortal praise
Whom I have loved, who have given me, dared with me
High secrets, and in darkness knelt to see
The inenarrable godhead of delight?
Love is a flame:—we have beaconed the world's night.
A city:—and we have built it, these and I.
An emperor:—we have taught the world to die.
So, for their sakes I loved, ere I go hence,
And the high cause of Love's magnificence,
And to keep loyalties young, I'll write those names
Golden for ever, eagles, crying flames,

136

And set them as a banner, that men may know,
To dare the generations, burn, and blow
Out on the wind of Time, shining and streaming. . . .
These I have loved:
    White plates and cups, clean-gleaming,
Ringed with blue lines; and feathery, faery dust;
Wet roofs, beneath the lamp-light; the strong crust
Of friendly bread; and many-tasting food;
Rainbows; and the blue bitter smoke of wood;
And radiant raindrops couching in cool flowers;
And flowers themselves, that sway through sunny
hours,
Dreaming of moths that drink them under the
moon;
Then, the cool kindliness of sheets, that soon
Smooth away trouble; and the rough male kiss
Of blankets; grainy wood; live hair that is
Shining and free; blue-massing clouds; the keen
Unpassioned beauty of a great machine;
The benison of hot water; furs to touch;
The good smell of old clothes; and others such—
The comfortable smell of friendly fingers,
Hair's fragrance, and the musty reek that lingers
About dead leaves and last year's ferns. . . .
         Dear names,
And thousand other throng to me! Royal flames;
Sweet water's dimpling laugh from tap or spring;
Holes in the ground; and voices that do sing;
Voices in laughter, too; and body's pain,
Soon turned to peace; and the deep-panting train;
Firm sands; the little dulling edge of foam
That browns and dwindles as the wave goes home;
And washen stones, gay for an hour; the cold
Graveness of iron; moist black earthen mould;
Sleep; and high places; footprints in the dew;
And oaks; and brown horse-chestnuts, glossy-new;

And new-peeled sticks; and shining pools on
grass;—
All these have been my loves. And these shall pass,
Whatever passes not, in the great hour,
Nor all my passion, all my prayers, have power
To hold them with me through the gate of Death.
They'll play deserter, turn with the traitor breath,
Break the high bond we made, and sell Love's trust
And sacramented covenant to the dust.
——Oh, never a doubt but, somewhere, I shall
wake,
And give what's left of love again, and make
New Friends, now strangers. . . .
                              But the best I've known
Stays here, and changes, breaks, grows old, is blown
About the winds of the world, and fades from
brains
Of living men, and dies.
                              Nothing remains.
O dear my loves, O faithless, once again
This one last gift I give: that after men
Shall know, and later lovers, far-removed,
Praise you, 'All these were lovely'; say, 'He loved.'

Rupert Brooke wrote that in Mataica in 1914, and you
used it to sum up your thesis. I guess the mean question
I want to ask is: Name your loves.
BUCHANAN: Oh gosh. I know some rather good poets
who have tried that. Mark Van Doren is one.
WOFFORD: It makes you want to write your own poem?
BUCHANAN: Yes, but I couldn't begin. The point I was
making is that these are all very concrete things.
WOFFORD: That's right. You began your thesis saying:
"I am ambitious enough to seek a general methodology
not merely for this or that discipline but rather an or-
ganon of intellectual imagination. This essay takes this

task seriously yet I hope lightly." And half way through I notice you turn to art and say, "Art seduces by illusion." Then you end with this poem, which is very concrete and full of the world of phenomena and art. I've been probing beyond your Socratic center to see if there are other centers, like the fine arts or the natural world—other loves that educate you?

BUCHANAN: Yes. You see this is based on an interest I had in value theory earlier. Value is a terrible term that's come into modern philosophy. It worried me a good deal, especially in the social sciences. My thesis at Oxford, quite different from this Harvard one, was about that, and this is the remainder. It's about transcendentals, especially two of them, good and evil. These are predictable of everything. That means that value—good—is everywhere. So this particular transcendental builds a world, a teleological world for us. The whole universe is filled with goods and evils, of mixed kinds capable of formulation in various ways.

If I were writing this thesis now, this poem would be weak. I should want something like Dante on love, to take in the whole universe. You know the Seventeenth Canto of the Purgatorio, which would be the exact middle of the whole Divine Comedy, had Dante's theory of natural love—the goods of the universe and how they are ordered. This is an extraordinary place in Dante. I'm sure he put it in the center purposely. He didn't do many things by mistake. This would be where I'd be now on all this. It's a much bigger thing than I ever dreamed of when I started.

WOFFORD: Last night Stringfellow Barr pointed out that though Gandhi talked of love and non-violence as the means, when he came to the meaning of life in his autobiography. He called it *The Story of My Experiments with Truth.*

BUCHANAN: Truth is another transcendental. You see

what this business of the transcendental good does to the way we talk about love at present—you know, the "loving community" and "let's love each other" and a whole lot of things of that sort that is pretty weak stuff. We ought to love all good things, needless to say God, but nature, too. The whole world is loveable and if you don't wake up to that the human side is weak and silly. We're doing too much of this loving each other business at present, it seems to me. I mean we're talking about it too much—we're not doing it very well, and won't do it well as long as we don't see the full range. Put it another way. You're not going to love the world unless you love God. That's the key to it, the center of the whole thing.

WOFFORD: The idea of God, or God manifest in this universe full of ends?

BUCHANAN: Whatever God you can approach. The point is that God is the formality under which you can love the world.

WOFFORD: I'm listening hard.

BUCHANAN: I'm talking hard. You know St. Thomas's order of love. Number one, you love God. Number two, you love yourself, your own soul. Number three, you love your neighbor's soul. Number four, you love your neighbor's body. Number five, you love your own body. These are the orders of charity—the true relations.

WOFFORD: And is that a ladder you start to climb from the bottom by loving a person? You know Meredith's line: "She is as my heart first awaking whispered the world was." Or is it really the other way? The world is as my heart first awaking whispered she was. What first wakes you up.

BUCHANAN: Plato's ladder of love would be like this: bodies, souls, institutions, laws, and so on, up to beauty. The ladders of love, the itinerary of love—this business is various, of course.

The Fine Arts and
the Liberal Arts

WOFFORD: To what extent do you get awakened by the world of beauty and art? You said art seduces us. Is this a seduction that leads to the kind of love that is the center of education?

BUCHANAN: There was a stage we all went through on this—a period when a good many philosophers of my age and time thought aesthetics, poetry, the novel, things of this sort, were the only way we were going to revive our own intellectual life. I taught aesthetics for quite a number of years when I first began teaching. We took it very seriously. This was for me not just a little side show in philosophy; it was the new world coming through.

WOFFORD: The fine arts, too?

BUCHANAN: Oh yes. The fine arts, and, if you like, nature. This is still a great theme, and still a viable road to take. But it proved illusory for most of us. At some point there was a great disenchantment, a great frustration, a disillusionment on this road. The arts didn't take us where we wanted to go.

WOFFORD: Are you sure? I think the arts are very important to the groping and searching that the coming generation is engaged in.

BUCHANAN: You certainly are turning up dirty questions. I have another theory about this. My disillusionment with this whole route came to a sort of a climax when I discovered what I now think of as the liberal arts. There's a very funny piece of history here which is still mysterious to me. The liberal arts existed in the many forms and revolutions they have gone through and the rebuildings of them from some time around the first century or possibly B.C. a little bit. But there was a break in them around the time of the Renaissance. There was a rebellion against them, inside the academy, and it took the form of establishing the fine arts. The fine arts had never existed as separate in people's minds. It's as if the liberal arts began to break up and people began saving splinters. The fine arts are splinters of the liberal arts. They should belong to them.

WOFFORD: How were they integrated before the break-up in the Renaissance?

BUCHANAN: They were involved in various ways. They were parts of all the arts. Beauty is an aspect of all this. Art in connection with beauty is a useful art. It's what a maker does, anyone that makes things—makes poems, makes chairs, makes anything. There's beauty connected with this. And as that ladder of love shows, in institutions, too. As long as there was a kind of intellectual integrity in the liberal arts, this was there as an integral part of it, with poetry always on the edge of being something else. Poetics was always a thing to talk about separately. But with the Renaissance the revolt was complete, and the fine arts, no longer liberal arts, set themselves up. I suppose this was around the time of Leonardo. He must have had something to do with this. I don't mean he was a rebel. On the contrary, he saw all these together, but for him it was a whole big array, and he was as much a fine artist as he was an industrial artist as he was a liberal artist. He was all these things in some funny way, and very much a man of tradition, not a rebel. He fulfills T.S. Eliot's notion about tradition and original talent. Leonardo was so deeply in a tradition that almost everything he did was an innovation.

SCHICKELE: That was the genius of the Renaissance.

WOFFORD: How would you bring them back together?

BUCHANAN: You can't do it at present without finding

out more about the liberal arts. That's the secret of it. If you could ever get ahold of that, the way we were trying to do at St. John's, I think they would then come back. We did a funny trick: we said we will leave the fine arts out of the curriculum, but they will be the number one extracurricular activity. And music became that—at one point it almost took over the college. This was happening at all colleges—the fine arts were taking the place of the liberal arts everywhere. Sarah Lawrence and all these places were doing this. We had a real fight at this point. Not an open fight, but a scramble—for we were not doing the liberal arts well enough to keep the fine arts in place. We all loved music and we had some swell people doing it, but I know my own son practically dropped the program and went in for music for quite a long time. And everything was in it, you see; in a curious way there was a strong intellectual content. And music, you know, is the third member of the quadrivium.

WOFFORD: I can see your mathematical eye. The quadrivium in which music was one category dealt with mathematics?

BUCHANAN: Yes, sure. That's a test of the liberal arts and the fine arts right there. To call music a liberal art now is funny antiquarian stuff, or even magic. To say that Mozart understood what he was doing in terms of mathematics is to appall people. They say, "Oh, for God's sake! That's the worst side of Mozart." And Bach the same way. But when they were writing they knew what they were saying in mathematical terms and in terms of sounds, too, all the time. They're about the last ones that did, of course. Music's now become the expression of the emotions. (Wofford is called away.)

SCHICKELE: I have one question about art I'd like to ask. You were talking about the Socratic belief in every individual having the oracle within him. I was wondering if you had ever considered art as one of the ways in which that oracle either could be reached or one of the ways in which it could be expressed. In other words how does the man get the oracle out of him? Is art one of the expressions of this oracle in our mind? oracle in our mind?

BUCHANAN: Very much. It's sort of the beginning of it. That is, I'd say this is one of the great ways in. This is Plato, very strongly, when you talk this way, because beauty was for him, as it was later for the medievals, a seduction—a seduction towards the intellect, towards truth, towards good.

SCHICKELE: And also perhaps a seduction away from going back down into the cave?

BUCHANAN: Quite. The way out. Very much. And now it's taken on a heavy burden. I think that's one of the reasons it's crumpling. It's trying to do so much, in this time of struggle, that it buckles under the burden.

SCHICKELE: Do you think it needs the support of the liberal arts?

BUCHANAN: Very much.

SCHICKELE: The structure of the liberal arts?

BUCHANAN: Yes, and, as you're suggesting, a good many fine artists realize this now.

SCHICKELE: You said you had contemplated writing a novel once. Was this an impulse towards beauty or towards clarity?

BUCHANAN: That's not a dilemma, I shouldn't think. I was doing something a little more primitive. I was trying to find the right mode of expression. The ordinary writing of philosophy seemed to me barbarian, and so many of the novels are awful. I was hunting for something in between, and, of course, drama is the strongest of any of them. But I had great hopes for the novel, too. Of course, I realized I couldn't write fiction very well. I haven't any gift for that, I don't think. I've never really tried it, but I don't believe I'd be any good at getting characters or dialogue. I don't think I have the right ear, the right feel for it. I wrote one chapter and gave up, not merely because I was frustrated by what I'd tried but other things seemed more important.

Music, Mathematics and Emotion

SCHICKELE: What was your association with music before the advent of the phonograph?

BUCHANAN: I took lessons the way most people do.

SCHICKELE: Piano?

BUCHANAN: Yes. I didn't get very far. Mother played the piano pretty well. And quite a lot of church music. I was a very churchy young fellow in my early years.

SCHICKELE: Did you master notation enough so that you were able to indulge your interest in mathematics by making a mathematical analysis of Bach?

BUCHANAN: Not strictly speaking. As you know, it isn't a very good mathematical notation. Our modern music shows that it isn't aware that it's mathematical.

SCHICKELE: A lot of modern compositions are written on graph paper.

BUCHANAN: I know, and probably ought to be. But you would have to make over the instruments a bit. It would be a real revolution, to bring this back to a mathematical basis. And of course there is a thing that the Pythagoreans discovered, a real discrepancy in the scale. It's something we have to fudge on the piano; the piano tuner knows what this is. He has to fudge a particular range of notes in order to make them go together because they are not strictly mathematical.

SCHICKELE: That's the meaning of the well-tempered clavier.

BUCHANAN: That's right.

SCHICKELE: The tempering is the evening out of the diatonic scale.

BUCHANAN: Right. This is very interesting. I'm claiming too much for this mathematical background for music. I don't know how far back it goes. The Pythagoreans knew it—it's that far back. And of course all the modes and the scales and everything are puzzles in this, so that mathematics has never been too smoothly applicable. It made Plato say that metaphysically there's a principle of error in the universe because these things didn't fit together very well.

SCHICKELE: Has the seeming irony ever fascinated you in the fact that music is in a way the most mathematical of the arts as well as being the most affective?

JACQUELINE GRENNAN: I'm interested in another aspect. Music is the most communicative to many people's notion and there's also the other intuition that the universal language is in some way going to be mathematical. I know some physicists who are already beginning to play with the notion of a science called anticryptography, as a way to communicate with beings on other planets. The notion would be to make the code as simple as you can, and at least the first hunches are that when you start to think that way, it will be essentially mathematical.

BUCHANAN: This is all relevant. High emotional content and mathematical sounds paradoxical, doesn't it? It isn't. This is the release, you see. If you want to turn on the emotions, then be intellectual. It's the only way that works. Most people think it's the opposite: you want to be emotional or passionate you'd better stop thinking. But it's quite the contrary. You know the reversal that T.S. Eliot made on this? The spirit giveth and the letter giveth away. It's an interesting reversal. He's not denying the truth of the other. But he's saying this one is just as true. Now this spoils all of our argument, doesn't it? He was very strong on this. I got to know Eliot and we used to talk about this a good deal. It's a great thing to think about. I don't know how far you want to take it. But it's obvious there are two things here. You've got to have both spirit and letter. Now it can be you're missing the spirit—that's what the anomie, the alienation is all about at present—but it can be the spirit is looking for the letter. No?

Paradox and Dogma

GRENNAN: Do you see the sense of paradox as a controlling center for your thinking?

BUCHANAN: Yes, of course, that's good old Platonic doctrine. Contradiction. You mean it in that sense, don't you? That's the beginning of all intellectual awakening, it seems to me.

GRENNAN: The only way I can read the Gospel is that He taught that way. He never really gave a flat statement but He seemingly talks in polarities all the time because they are the only way you can save man from a formula solution.

BUCHANAN: Right. This is Plato, you know—this is in *The Republic,* there's a whole section on this, on what the intellectual awakening is based on. It's the discovery of contradiction, always.

GRENNAN: May I ask—if it's an unfair question just don't answer, but I've been asking it a lot of myself and of other people. You talk often of God, and then mercifully say that you don't want to define that concept. Do you have any conviction that we will have a self-conscious awareness of ourselves a couple of centuries from now, you and I?

BUCHANAN: You're really talking about the hereafter?

GRENNAN: I want it in concrete terms, though. I want to know whether you believe I will be self-consciously aware of my existence two centuries from now.

BUCHANAN: The terms are bad, aren't they?

GRENNAN: Is Plato self-consciously aware of his existence right now?

BUCHANAN: I don't believe I know. The eternity and time business—you can't jump it—even sempiternal is in between there somewhere.

GRENNAN: What do you mean "sempiternal?"

BUCHANAN: Always existing. Eternity means without any time. Sempiternal means existing in time, endlessly. Now those two are related in some funny way, and that sounds like what you're talking about. Two centuries from now—you're talking about sempiternal. And I'm not sure that's part of the immortality business at all.

GRENNAN: What does immortality say to you?

BUCHANAN: It says that my soul, the part of it that matters, exists out of time. Now and always. No?

GRENNAN: I think I would have more sense of wonder without it.

BUCHANAN: Yes. I'm awfully sure of this, that the Incarnation is much more important. In that sense Christmas is more important than Easter.

SCHICKELE: Is this because creation and existence are more important than redemption?

BUCHANAN: Yes. Who am I to say, but it seems to me the Incarnation is *the* central thing. It's central to the whole sacramental system, central to the whole meaning of the new dispensation—to getting the law and the spirit and everything straightened out.

SCHICKELE: You say most people think the resurrection is the most important. Is the church responsible for the corruption this represents? Or is it simply that people feel, because of guilt or something else, the importance of the redemption more than they do the importance of their own existence? I don't know if I'm making myself clear.

BUCHANAN: Yes, I think you are, but it's a terribly complicated question. It seems to me you're asking what was the cause of the deception?

SCHICKELE: Yes.

BUCHANAN: This is some degradation in the teaching of the doctrine. Now who did this? The parish priest, you'd be tempted to say—or the pastor of my Congregational Church—or somebody. They didn't know these doctrines. They passed them on very badly. I never guessed what they meant when I was a child and here I was a very devout Christian. But I never got any intelligibility in what was being said. I had my own version of it, but I was frightened of some of it. As a matter of fact there was a period when I wouldn't take communion at all because I was horrified by it. Eating the body of Christ—what's this all about? And no one could tell me. When we moved during this period, I went into a city church and made a point of saying that if I kept in the church I wouldn't take communion. This was a crisis for the church committee. I just couldn't take it.

SCHICKELE: Your religious life seems to have been intellectually very alive most of your life. Was there ever a period of extreme doubt?

BUCHANAN: Oh yes, about the time I went to college I was pretty well washed up in the whole thing.

GRENNAN: Has there ever been a time when you consciously submerged your skepticism about religion?

BUCHANAN: I think I saved all of it. The dogma is the thing to be questioned. That's the way to keep dogmas alive. So it's important to be a skeptic, although I think I believe very deeply. But I want to question them all the time. I don't understand them yet.

GRENNAN: And don't expect to?

BUCHANAN: Not wholly, no. You know Maritain says that a mystery, a church mystery, is something that is capable of endless rational exploration. This seems to me to be quite true.

GRENNAN: I think he chisels sometimes.

BUCHANAN: I'm afraid he does, but this is a beautiful thing, and I hope it isn't chiseling. You were using the word exploration about it and I was agreeing.

The Fine Arts and the Divine Arts

GRENNAN: This fits with your notion of art, I think. The artist is supremely contemplative, and if a piece of art is really worthwhile you can keep contemplating and contemplating and contemplating it. I've been thinking that whoever or whatever God is, if we say he is infinite, he is able to be contemplated without end. If you tie this back to your theory of art—that it is the most beautiful and the most wondrous and the most capable of eliciting endless emotion inasmuch as it is intellectual—you know, the elegance of mathematics—I'm thinking this for the first time and trying to bring together your notion of art and mathematics and contemplation and the rational component: that's very exciting. All loves are like that, too, I think.

BUCHANAN: Right. Endless. You can put it that way, too. A good many of our attitudes about the fine arts are imitations of the mystic vision—I mean the beatific vision. The fine arts are an imitation of the divine arts. You see, that's the pun.

GRENNAN: You should in a sense be calling the divine arts a transcendent fine art.

BUCHANAN: Quite.

GRENNAN: That's too beautiful.

BUCHANAN: Did you ever know Sister Medaleva?

GRENNAN: I just met her.

BUCHANAN: I got to know her, and there was one occasion when Mortimer Adler and I had lunch with her and another sister in a very special dining room at St. Mary's College. This was the only time she ever acted proselytizing at all with me—a very beautiful occasion because she did it so well. She put the question pretty tightly, pretty hot. I told her that with all my backslidings and everything else, I thought I knew where the center was and on which circle I existed, and I wasn't too concerned, like some of the lower orders in heaven, about being closer. I accepted my position. It was distant from the center but I knew where it was, and to push this with me, in the sense of joining the Roman Catholic Church—which in some sense I ought to do—would be hypocrisy, a self-deception of a bad kind. I said, "I'm afraid it would just end up being an aesthetic business with me, if I did that, because I'm very susceptible to that." And she said, "Don't you realize that it is the genuine aesthetic experience?" I had no answer to this. I said it would be romantic for me to join the church and she said, Yes it's the great Romance.

GRENNAN: If they had just slipped a little—they should have lisped a little—but somebody ruined it by making it the genuine *ascetic* instead of *aesthetic* experience and the whole thing fell apart—the whole Puritan mess.

BUCHANAN: Right. Sister Medaleva was wonderful. I knew her some after that, but we never brought this up again; she knew she had said the right thing, and I knew she had too.

SCHICKELE: What do you think are the temptations of an intellectual life? Temptations in the sense Christ had temptations he felt he had to resist.

BUCHANAN: The temptations of the intellectual life of course are deployed and demonstrated to you in the whole Christian story. From Satan, the great temptation, down through Adam and Eve and all the rest—there are an endless number of them. The great one is wanting to be God—wanting to be omniscient.

LANDRUM: Is it a meaningful paradox to you that you are one of the most evident children of Eve—in your desire to know? And yet you consider her action a giving in to temptation?

BUCHANAN: You mean any intellectual curiosity?

LANDRUM: Yes.

BUCHANAN: Sure, this is one of the first great temptations—the great sin.

LANDRUM: But you obviously don't feel badly about having taken that course.

BUCHANAN: Yes, I do. I can even read this into the Bible. If you read that section carefully in Genesis about the Garden of Eden and what went on between the Devil and Eve, you will find the liberal arts in the middle of this. Wanting to know is the great sin, and I think it's always tragic, the beginning of a tragic episode in anything. Any piece of knowledge is the beginning of a tragic thing.

SCHICKELE: To say something is a sin or is tragic is not to say it should be avoided.

BUCHANAN: If you can. But this is original sin, that is, Eve and Adam having done this—this is where the myth gets us—we all have to do the same thing, in some way, because they did.

SCHICKELE: Having opted for the tragic, then what are the next temptations?

BUCHANAN: It's intellectual pride of all sorts and then

the curiosities of one kind or another. Some of this modern stuff—this group therapy and everything—seems to me a bad curiosity about people. You know there used to be a sense of privacy and dignity and everything else about this. Now you've got to know everything.

SCHICKELE: But you were saying great curiosity is sinful and tragic, too.

BUCHANAN: Yes. But we have to do it.

SCHICKELE: We don't have to do the other stuff?

BUCHANAN: Well we may. I'm not denying that we may have to do it now. We're in such a mess that possibly it's the only thing we can do. No, the sins are so concatenated, you know. There are an awful lot of them, and they're connected in almost necessary ways. I believe that to call a sin necessary is very heretical, but it's so damn near it I don't see any point in denying it.

SCHICKELE: Do you consider doubt a temptation?

BUCHANAN: Not very much. Doubt seems to me a kind of cure for a bad intellectual pride. This is very complex. I don't behave well under any of these things. I can't conform with my best ideas about these things. I've got very evil curiosities and I indulge them and do all sorts of things. (Wofford returns.)

The Academy and the City

LANDRUM: I'm curious about the geography of a modern university. I have a vague notion that the modern university is built on a medieval model, and the world is different now, so we ought to take into account its mobility and the mobility of students and professors. Could you explain where the Academy was in Athens and what it looked like?

153

BUCHANAN: There's very little known. There's a tree in Athens—the stump of a tree—that's said to be on the locale of the Academy. It's in the market district, a very low slum part of Athens at present. And that's all that's known about where it was. There are references to its having gardens and walks.

LANDRUM: We don't know whether it was a retreat?

BUCHANAN: It certainly was an old estate, the estate of some very rich Athenian. But how it got into Plato's hands and why and what he did with it, I don't know.

WOFFORD: You said earlier that Roger was asking for too drastic a thing when he said let's go all the way back to Socrates. But I take it Socrates wasn't ever in the place you are referring to.

BUCHANAN: The Academy is much later than Socrates. Socrates had already died. In a sense the Academy might have been a memorial to him.

WOFFORD: Did Socrates have much of a locus?

BUCHANAN: The dialogues give you locus.

WOFFORD: The dialogues took place all over, didn't they?

BUCHANAN: Gymnasium and market-place and outside the city walls. They were everywhere but always connected with the city. Socrates was a city man.

LANDRUM: Do you have any thoughts about whether the university should be a retreat, or whether making it a beautiful, quiet, aristocratic place may be giving in to the intellectual sin—a form of intellectual pride?

BUCHANAN: This may be a very important question you're asking, that is, what to do next about the damn business of the city and the university. They ought to be combined, I'm not sure you ought to take this too literally. For instance, I am not at all afraid of the ivory tower. There ought to be one. It ought to be cultivated. You agree, don't you?

LANDRUM: Yes, I think there ought to be a place where you could go.

BUCHANAN: A lot of people condemn anything that's ivory tower. They say those people are not connected with reality. To hell with that! You're as much connected with reality when you're thinking as you are when you are in the marketplace. The ivory tower should be a much bigger institution than it is at present. There aren't any ivory towers practically, now. And it certainly shouldn't be condemned. Just where this great function should be done, geographically, I don't know. I am very much interested in these new towns that are being built around a university. It may be the only way the cities can come back to life. Do you know about Columbia, the new town between Washington and Baltimore?

WOFFORD: Roger and I were in on a planning session for the college of Columbia, but it fell a little short of your description.

BUCHANAN: I haven't heard the latest news, but when it first was being proposed, it seemed like a brilliant idea. When we discussed it here practically everybody in our meeting, 30 people, most of them technicians, were immediately interested. Now there's a good deal of this kind of thinking.

WOFFORD: I thought you were saying maybe we should not take it literally, but now you're saying take it literally and combine the city and the university.

BUCHANAN: Yes, now I am. As a present emergency, I can see the university saving the city and vice versa.

GRENNAN: I've played with the pun *univer-city*. That's what a university should be.

BUCHANAN: If you're asking what will bring us to a recognition of the function of a city, I say a university will do it, where the university is the center of it, the main activity. If you make it strong—that the industry of this city is going to be the university.

GRENNAN: The maker of the city.

BUCHANAN: And what the city makes.

LANDRUM: But how do you get a university that slaves can come to and learn to be free? A university can so easily be a sort of playground for the aristocracy.

BUCHANAN: The poor rich people ought to have their place, too. I don't know how to think about this question you're continually raising. That is, I've lost my Marxian view of the proletariat and the aristocracy, and there's a confusion in my mind now about these divisions, the rich and the poor, and the aristocrats and hoi polloi. I'm not settling for Reinhold Niebuhr's view that the world is always run by an elite, or by a minority as he says, but I don't believe that pouring everything into one big pot is going to do anything. We've got to have more structure.

LANDRUM: You do still see the world divided into civilized and uncivilized men —

BUCHANAN: No, I don't believe I do. I see most everybody partly civilized, partly not, partly free and partly slave, in different ways, in different patterns.

WOFFORD: One of your students at St. John's said the one thing that keeps buzzing in his head that he attributes to you is the line: "All the world is relations."

BUCHANAN: This is one of these transcendental tricks. You put two or three transcendentals together and you get relations out of them, and relations build the world—as one and many, universal and particular and so on did. Combinations of them build your world.

WOFFORD: Now we know the name of your magic.

LANDRUM: Are Western ideas in the Western classics the only kind of magic? If the classics are the curriculum to make a free man at the university level, that leaves out the elementary schools and the high schools. Take, for example, the Negro ghetto in the city. What is the curriculum for Negro children that would come out of their own tradition and be liberating to them, as the classics would be to the aristocracy coming into the university? Would your thinking lead you in a search for the classics of that community?

BUCHANAN: I'm not stuck on the classics at all. We took the great books for a very special purpose: let's try these at St. John's until we find what a college should really be. There's no magic about this. We were trying to invent a college at that point, the way Harris is now, and these were some special things we wanted to use. The classics are important, but I was immediately embarrassed when we got to be exclusively connected with the classics and the classical tradition.

LANDRUM: You no longer believe the classics are the best manifestation of the tradition?

BUCHANAN: Almost by definition they are—the great books are the best works, the master works, of the liberal arts, but there's a lot more to be said about them.

LANDRUM: Do you understand the question I'm asking?

BUCHANAN: I'm afraid I don't. You're asking what would be the right medium for teaching Negro children. I don't know. I'd like to know. I think it ought to be found out, and fast. The Headstart stuff ought to be discovering this. For instance, I am pretty sure that children of a very tender age ought to be learning languages, as they do in most countries. We're very backward in that. And I'm very sure that kids of a very tender age have very special mathematical ability. These two—language and mathematics—are the grand roads and ought to be begun early. But I don't know what form they should take.

LANDRUM: The Negro kids I know have a brilliant language. The dilemma is the two traditions of language in which they are caught.

BUCHANAN: But it does separate them from the rest

of the community pretty well, doesn't it?

GRENNAN: Or it separates us from them.

BUCHANAN: Both ways, yes. This is one of those awful questions: Should we make a common language the basis for community? Perhaps not, yet you look at India or Nigeria and it looks pretty bad if you don't have one. If you do the sentimental thing, like the Irish with Gaelic, or the revived Hebrew in Israel, it does awful things to the people—yet wonderful things, too. I studied enough Hebrew to know what a wonderful thing it is doing. What's the word for electricity? Well you find it in Ezekiel: the lightning above the throne of God. In order to get the sewers properly labeled, in the blueprint of the sewers of Tel Aviv, they had to get one of their best poets to work with an engineer, and the poet dug out old Hebrew words and did things to them to make them describe pipe joints.

LANDRUM: The lack of answers leads me to the notion that at any given point with a set of people a curriculum is at worst negotiated and at best there is a dialogue about it.

BUCHANAN: At St. John's we had an instruction committee continually working on the curriculum, revising it, changing it. We were going on with this in a very powerful way. Then the war came and took our best people, and we never got back to it. It's never come to life again. Later, when we were going to start a college in Massachusetts, we decided to have a three part affair. One would be an undergraduate college; second, a county-wide adult education program; and number three would be a curriculum research committee. And we were to rotate the faculty in those three things, in order to keep a faculty alive. You know how they all die. I remember I said to Sister Madaleva when I was visiting St. Mary's, how do you keep your faculty alive? And she said—we were just passing a chapel:

"Here's one thing. Every morning, the Eucharist." And she said, "The next thing I can think of is that I hang maybaskets on their doors on Mayday."

GRENNAN: The second answer was more important than the first, because if you go look, the chapel's still there, and Madaleva isn't and the college is now as dead as a doornail.

BUCHANAN: I'd guess that. She was a very special person and she was in the college in lots of ways. But how do you keep a faculty—how do you keep an institution from going wrong? We were very much concerned about this. The curriculum research committee would be the revolutionary committee, the permanent revolutionary committee, and it would come out of the experience of teaching adults, which helps an awful lot. Go out and teach some adults and see what you're up to—it changes your life a good deal. How many adults did you teach in Nigeria?

LANDRUM: About a third of my students were adults.

BUCHANAN: Then you know what I'm talking about, you know what this does to you. Do you miss it?

LANDRUM: I miss teaching, yes.

BUCHANAN: Teaching itself, teaching youngsters, ought to do this, but it doesn't. I think that's mainly what's the trouble now. Teaching is a dead art.

WOFFORD: Teaching is more alive with adults, you think, though adult education everywhere has been such a sorry story of failure?

BUCHANAN: Yes, adult education hasn't been good enough. That's what we were hoping to do—a saturation job, as we used to call it, in Berkshire County, Massachusetts. That was a county twenty-five miles each way, square, and had very interesting institutions in it to help this whole thing. We thought we could do a complete job and make it permanent. The awful thing about adult education is that people in it have to be mendicants

and itinerants. You have to really give up all your se-
curities in order to be a good adult teacher. No institution will support you.

SCHICKELE: Let's pursue that question. I keep telling
Harris the most important thing about a Socratic seminar is the Socrates himself, the leader. And thinking
about Socrates' own life, you know he had a nagging
wife—he was essentially alone. Thomas Mann has a
statement that you cannot hope to take a single leaf
from the tree of art without paying for it with your
whole life. In all of this there is a sense of the necessity
of some kind of sacrifice of life to instill and create
life, whether you do it by being a teacher or whether
you do it by being an artist. Is this perhaps one of the
reasons why education has become so difficult, because
we find so few people who are willing to be that free
and make that kind of sacrifice?

BUCHANAN: I remember asking Alec Meiklejohn in
the days when the University of California was having
its trouble with the loyalty oath. "What's really wrong
there, Alec?" He said, "It's simple: too high salaries."

GRENNAN: What did he mean?

BUCHANAN: It was such a bad show they put on. They
didn't stand up to their own regents or the investigating
committee or anything else. The faculty—except for 50
or so of them who resigned—just couldn't do anything.
It was safer that way. There was no academic freedom
shown in that faculty except by the people that left it.

GRENNAN: They had been bought?

BUCHANAN: Yes, and Alec usually didn't give this
simple an answer. He wasn't an economic determinist,
but he said, "In this case I'm afraid that's all there is
to it. They are just too cozy and happy and complacent
to take on the real job." This means they weren't teaching well. I think that's the trouble with them now—just
bad teaching at Berkeley. No one says so, but I'm pretty

sure it is. Again, I don't mean to be blaming individuals. It's an institutional situation.

LANDRUM: They weren't teaching well because they weren't living well?

BUCHANAN: The reasons why they weren't teaching well are very complex. They were too affluent, but it's also an enormous institution. The trouble with most of these places is they are growing like mad, and no one has been able to understand or guide them in any safe or effective way. Any institution growing as fast as our educational institutions are growing now is going to have awful troubles, no matter how good your management is or anything else. When you look at it this way it isn't surprising that they're having awful difficulties and misunderstanding themselves. You don't have to go into any special causes for the breakdown—just the sheer size and weight of the enterprise, and the acceleration of the enterprise, is enough to explain it all. And you're stepping right in the middle of it, sir.

WOFFORD: The whirlwind, Robert Hutchins said. Shall I ask you next time what you're going to write your novel about?

BUCHANAN: Well, not this time, I wanted to say and I'd better say it now, that the thing I dislike about this interview business is I can't do the thing I enjoy the most, and that is turn questions around on the other people.

WOFFORD: Try it.

BUCHANAN: Next time I shall.

WOFFORD: Next year in Jerusalem.

VI

NO DOCTRINES FOR SALE

[January 24, 1968]

Demons and the Beatific Vision

WOFFORD: David Schickele accuses you of leaving the arts out of your grand design.

BUCHANAN: The fine arts?

WOFFORD: Yes.

BUCHANAN: He leaves out all the others.

WOFFORD: But he was pleased with your talk last time about paradise, God, immortality, and sex—while I was out of the room. Would you give me a summary?

BUCHANAN: We were talking about the fine arts being imitations of the divine arts, and the beauty of this. They have been known as the fine arts ever since the Renaissance, but the ancients never recognized them as separate from the useful arts or the intellectual arts; they were always part of those. Why should they have split off from the liberal arts, at some point or other around the early Renaissance? I have never heard a satisfactory answer to that, but we can make some guesses. It was a time when the Church and the sacraments were falling into less repute, and the fine arts were substitutes for the sacraments.

You can take this one step further. The beatific vision is in beauty. Actually the words have no connection at all, but there is a relationship between the beatific vision, as described by Dante in the *Paradiso*, and all the theories we have now about beauty—so-called aesthetic theory. It used to be intellectual. That is, the beatific vision or beauty used to have an intellectual content, but that's lost. Works of art used to have intellectual content and were appreciated for that, but as the fine arts developed they lost that for the most part, and became stimuli for emotions. And people think their sentiments are being trained by beautiful objects, works of art, and actually practising the arts. This is a degradation of the whole enterprise. I don't feel like reforming it, because these are very much going concerns now, even on a big industrial scale. Productions or reproductions of great works of art, even in music, are a commercial business, and insofar as they are distributed, I suppose it's good for people. But our understanding of the arts dwindles all the time, and becomes less and less significant and less and less important.

Now, what Schickele was worrying about is another thing: he's worrying about the separation of the two.

WOFFORD: Let's go back to the emotions and the *Divine Comedy* and the idea of love. I'm doing this in Schickele's name because at the end of his article on the Peace Corps he said that the truth was beyond him and the only thing that cuts a little ice is affection. The trip many people are taking today, or trying to take, or hoping to take, seems to me to go up from the emotions and the sentiments and esthetic stimulation to love.

BUCHANAN: That's another thing that's been destroyed. Love being, as Dante says, the thing that makes the world go round, is destroyed now, too, as an entity itself. It's become a matter of sentiments, emotions, and so forth. A love that is fundamental to all the emotions, and to all the knowledge we have, is quite another thing. In Dante it's the top of the whole thing. God is the object of knowledge *and* of love—the complete object of those two things. That is, everything anyone ever loved exists in God in some way. Reaching the beatific vision, which is the vision of God, is the climax. Even the theologians now have about five different names for love. I won't be able to remember them: there's *Eros* and *Agape*—those are the two famous ones—and *Philia.* People make very sharp distinctions between them— even Martin Luther King does—but this seems to me a very bad thing to do, because it's all one thing.

WOFFORD: I realize with my own children that parental love is certainly mixed with strains of sexuality. I know that without Freud. And in the love of my wife, in addition to sexuality, there's very strong philial love. *Philia* means brotherly?

BUCHANAN: Friendship. It's a very strong word in Greek. I remember when I was teaching some philosophy at Springfield College about 1954, we were reading Plato, and I referred to *Philia*—I guess it was a point about the word philosophy, the love of wisdom—and a Greek girl came up at the end of the class and said, "You know *philia* doesn't mean love in Greek." I said, "No?" She said, "It means kissing." It's a wholly physical word now. It had none of the old meaning at all to her. I hadn't known that, but it's like them—I mean it's like languages to do that, and it's like the Greeks to have done it to their language.

WOFFORD: You said earlier, when we were talking about Socrates, that homosexuality among the Greeks pervaded the dialogues and clarified them.

BUCHANAN: Did I say "clarify" them?

WOFFORD: I'm not sure you said "clarified," but whoever typed the transcript typed "clarified," and it wasn't clear to me.

BUCHANAN: I probably did. That isn't quite the right word for it. It illuminates it in some curious way. There is an atmosphere, and a big part of it was homosexuality. Probably the dialogues wouldn't have happened unless there had been that in the situation. Socrates makes fun of it all the time, and takes it seriously at the same time.

WOFFORD: Why wouldn't there have been the dialogue without it?

BUCHANAN: The kind of attention, and respect, and affection in the dialogues is not a sexual business very much but it's homosexual, if you want to put it that way. It's not just friendship. This is a kind of community bond. Again you find in Plato, many times, very short sentences in which *philia* is used, and he means by this a curious sentiment and love relationship of a very complex kind. This is a basis for the political state, it was for the Greeks. We'd find this a little difficult to put that way but it comes through Christianity in a funny way. Aristotle's remarks of this kind are taken by St. Thomas and made into Christian charity. *Charis*—that's another word for love.

WOFFORD: Last night I was telling some of your friends—former St. John's students or colleagues—that we thought your collected writings that Steve Benedict, John Van Doren and I are trying to edit ought to be entitled *Truth, the Aim of Education,* and we got into a dispute as to whether truth was an adequate description of what you were all about. The other camp was saying Love. They felt you had raised more questions about the nature of love than anybody they knew. I should add that they saw yours as a very abstract fleshless love, yet very direct and passionate, and they loved you. I guess this sounds like the end of the *Symposium* where they go to sleep talking about comedy and tragedy. Was that a question?

BUCHANAN: Not one I can answer. No, I wouldn't know. I recognize the categories.

WOFFORD: I've left out a few, I suppose.

BUCHANAN: Yes. It was another one that used to worry me at St. John's. There was a period when I was Dean and people used to come to me and talk to someone that wasn't me. I used to try to stop them, and say, "Look, you're talking to someone over my shoulder, here. It's not me you're talking to at all." That's a funny thing that happens to officials. You probably know about that already; you certainly will as you go along with your work. Any operating concern has this as a kind of parasentimental structure.

WOFFORD: How have you handled this? You certainly have this charismatic affect for many people.

BUCHANAN: I'm not much aware of having it. I know I'm very attached to some people and some of them are to me. This funny thing at St. John's, where it was very painful—I don't know exactly what was happening there. It wasn't wholly the Dean. It was something else, perhaps the author of the program, or something puffed up too much. I used to tell people to stop it, but I was never successful.

WOFFORD: You're accused of slapping people down pretty hard when they carry it too far.

BUCHANAN: Yes, I think I've done that. I think I've hurt people very much sometimes by just smashing through it, saying "Nonsense!" You can't handle them. You don't know what's going on.

WOFFORD: I'm pushing this because you've been talking about the younger generation, and I think love is an important aspect of where they are. I've been reading Norman O. Brown's *Love's Body*, an imaginative book that goes off in flashes. In good part it is an attack on the splitting of love into all the different kinds. I don't know whether he helps to understand it, but many of the young people in ferment are reaching for this.

BUCHANAN: This could be a very strong thing. The distinctions between kinds of love are very elusive.

WOFFORD: What do we do? How do we include these questions in the curriculum?

BUCHANAN: There are some rather important books that deal with it, you know. The philosophy of love is a great topic, one of the great traditions. It begins I suppose with *The Symposium* and runs through some very great things in the Middle Ages. It's the combination of intellect and the will—the object of the intellect is truth; the object of the will is the good; when these two operate together you have love. This is, of course, the basis for any good ethic. Then it comes into later philosophical stuff. Spinoza had a lot to say about it, and Schopenhauer on another side, and Kant. I don't know of any modern philosopher who's done a real job on this, except possibly Whitehead, and this isn't his best line. But as in the case of other things, we're undergoing a dissolution of a lot of categories. These things have been talked about in certain terms, and these are all breaking up. We've got to have some new ones. We can do this by a combination of what the youngsters are saying—what the beatniks and the hippies are doing—and a good literary understanding. Of course poetry's about this very often.

WOFFORD: There isn't much poetry in the St. John's curriculum?

BUCHANAN: Dante, Homer, Milton, Shakespeare— pretty well represented!

WOFFORD: Any poetry for the nineteenth and twentieth centuries?

BUCHANAN: No, because there's no great poetry in the nineteenth and twentieth century. I realize that's a sweeping remark to make, but I think it's true.

WOFFORD: Yet you said earlier you find Eliot and a

lot of other poems playing a large role in your thinking.

BUCHANAN: Oh, yes. The poets are important people. They talk a certain way which is very important. But I don't believe you can call their work really great. Now we're talking about another thing, of course: What's a great book? This doesn't mean that any little book is unimportant.

WOFFORD: One of the problems of the idea of great books is that this leaves out a great poem.

BUCHANAN: I just named about six of them—the greatest poetry in the world. You wouldn't argue that. Homer is not a great poet.

WOFFORD: Yes. A great poem and a great book. But there could be a great poem one page long.

BUCHANAN: Not really. I'm not saying one shouldn't read them, but I'm certainly saying they're not very great. They can be damned good. They can say a lot. But I wouldn't say you can have a really great piece of poetry without its being a long one—either dramatic or epic. But I think we're playing with terms. As a matter of fact there were occasions when we put readings in lyric poetry into the program at St. John's.

WOFFORD: Every Christmas Barr used to read *The Journey of the Magi.*

BUCHANAN: Oh, yes, we had some very familiar poems. Marvel's "In a Garden" got famous because of Bill Gorman's teaching of it, and the tutorials were doing a lot with poetry, French poetry particularly.

This great book business is funny. It was never argued, very much, at St. John's. I wanted to argue it, because I wanted to cut it down some, and there were occasions when I made a very strong plea, that we should really think about this again. But no one wanted to do it, for lots of reasons. We hadn't taught it enough. And the same was true about the question of the oriental books. I think oriental books ought to be in, but

168

I don't know just how important this is.

WOFFORD: How would you go about finding that out? What if our college wanted to do it?

BUCHANAN: I'd approve of it.

WOFFORD: How would you find out what oriental books to put in and how to do it?

BUCHANAN: This would be very difficult. Someone who is more or less familiar with them, for whom they are familiar pieces of furniture, might know how to do it. In the old days these seemed curious, distant things, that fascinated us. One way to understand your own religion is to read the oriental classics, but that doesn't mean you're understanding the oriental classics very well. T.S. Eliot and I agreed on this point. We always found when we went after these things, all we were doing was translating something of our own philosophical picture into oriental terms.

WOFFORD: You're sure that's not all the oriental authors were doing? I mean, is there an oriental tradition that is able to be found that hasn't been pervaded by the western?

BUCHANAN: No. At Oxford my friend Abdul Hamid used to get drunk on port wine, and he had stages he'd go through, of reminiscence and sentimental stuff, but I never could get him back to the one subject I wanted him to talk about, Indian philosophy. I'd come to Oxford because I had wanted to go for that, and I'd been disappointed in it. Finally one night he did talk Indian philosophy, and it turned out all to come from a famous philosopher at Oxford.

WOFFORD: You remember Gandhi claimed he didn't understand Hinduism until he went to England, and read Annie Besant. He read the *Bhagavad Gita* seriously first in English translation. Then he, a fairly westernized man, wrote his own translation of the *Gita* which was widely used in India.

BUCHANAN: This is probably truer than we think, and in that sense we've been stupid to be modest about it. I mean we ought to have gone at the oriental books simply and hard and we'd have cracked them.

WOFFORD: What we should do is get a few people starting to read them?

BUCHANAN: The best way to learn these things is to teach them. Just bring them into class and assign them and go ahead. Don't stand on your competence. When we said we were incompetent to do this with the oriental books, we didn't mean scholarly competence. We meant in some deep way we didn't have the imaginative and emotional context for really understanding them.

WOFFORD: Back to this question of love in the student-teacher relationship. In your account of your education, the chief example where there is that kind of strong influence is the way you talk about Alexander Meiklejohn.

BUCHANAN: An interesting thing about my relation with Meiklejohn is I never was a student of his. I suppose in one sense I was. There was a faculty seminar—an informal group that used to meet in Alex's study. We read Kant, and I was the youngest of the crowd. He wasn't really teaching in the ordinary sense, but in a very powerful sense of course he was. His presence was.

Who do I feel have been my teachers? There's a scattering of them. Some—I don't even remember their names—go back to primary and secondary school. There were several in high school, one or two in college.

This relationship is very difficult to describe: What a good teacher in relation to a student is. It isn't any one thing. I like the description Maritain gives, one mind brooding over another—worrying, and presenting, and withdrawing. The gentle side of the relationship is the important side—and brooding: the notion that you are bringing something to life inside the other mind.

WOFFORD: You thrust upon us, or people thrust upon you, this Socrates thing.

BUCHANAN: This is the construct of other people, I didn't plan it.

WOFFORD: But you've been unable to disentangle yourself from it for some time.

BUCHANAN: Right.

WOFFORD: It's very dangerous. I find myself alarmed by those who put a Don Quixote cast on me. It's not accurate. Of course I think the Socratic thing is accurate when it is applied to you.

To put a tragic lens on Socrates. I suppose the most tragic recognition for him would be concluding that the oracle was right, that he was the wisest man in Greece because he didn't find anybody who knew more than he, or didn't know as much about their ignorance as he did about his. That would be a very lonely discovery.

The Tragedy of Truth

BUCHANAN: I've just been reading a very funny book about Socrates, Kierkegaard's *Irony,* and it's all about Socrates, the whole thing. He sees Socrates as a kind of forerunner, a very destructive one. He collected the sophistry that was in Greece, transformed it in a certain way, and left them empty. Kierkegaard makes this one of the turning points in world history: when the Greeks were under this influence; the way they were and the way they went on. There's something in that. I think you have to take Socrates very literally when he said he didn't know.

WOFFORD: Do you have that feeling about yourself?

BUCHANAN: Yes. The last few years, very much. Before I've had doctrines for sale, the way everybody does, but I haven't got them anymore I don't think. And I find it very difficult to formulate any doctrine or anything I'd call the truth. But I have very strong negative feelings about it—because I know a lot of stuff that isn't the truth. It's a very funny experience. In a curious way I can't read my own life, or can't read the world anymore. I try to—I keep trying all the time, the way everybody does, but it doesn't come out for me. I don't know what it's all about. This is very disturbing to me.

WOFFORD: That's not a tragic recognition?

BUCHANAN: No. I don't feel that way about it. Perhaps I should! It may be something lacking in me.

WOFFORD: Well, a tragic recognition should tell you who you are, shouldn't it?

BUCHANAN: It should in some way, yes. But this doesn't do that to me. I'm not sure. It doesn't do it in the ordinary sense of discovering identity. That isn't what a tragic recognition does anyway. It isn't by itself a psychoanalytic or existential proposition.

WOFFORD: How do you distinguish it from a psychoanalytic proposition?

BUCHANAN: I always get corrected by psychoanalysts when I go into this, but I suppose the psychoanalytic proposition is finding your role in relation to other people, particularly the big father and mother and child images and so on, and getting it all into a form which releases you, and the other people too. This is very good. But "Know Thyself" in the Socratic sense means more than that. It is expanded; know what you are in relation to the whole world. I can't say much more. It's like the truth, it's very slippery.

WOFFORD: What's your reaction to *Truth, The Aim of Education* as the title for your writings, a play on Whitehead's *The Aims of Education*?

BUCHANAN: I agree with it. Mark Van Doren always accuses me of being the man concerned about the truth.

I recognize that. This almost frightens Mark. I've heard him say he was frightened by it.

WOFFORD: I'm for the title because it might frighten or take by surprise some of the people I want to read your collected works.

BUCHANAN: Yes.

WOFFORD: When I'm feeling tired and irritable, the one thing I know I can get a rise from, is to use the word truth in our planning discussions.

BUCHANAN: Yes, it gets people very sore, very angry, or very frightened. It's a terrible word at present—therefore a good word, I think, because this isn't a false fright. It's like the Biblical phrase, Fear of God.

WOFFORD: Does that phrase mean anything to you?

BUCHANAN: Fear of God? I think so. It's very close to this—very close to fear of the truth. The emotional reactions to these words are expressing something very important, I think. It is like the thing going on in Aristotle's "all men by nature desire to know"—which is another way of saying they seek the truth. This is the beginning of the whole educational enterprise, and the only real assumption that works with it.

WOFFORD: But you wouldn't put these two things together and consider the relation tragic? That truth is the aim—that is, was the aim—of your education and you think you don't know anything about it?

BUCHANAN: No, I don't think that is tragic.

WOFFORD: I'm pushing the tragic theme because I've been reading quite a bit about it as I re-read your stuff.

BUCHANAN: The tragic thing happens on a lower level than this. You find some particular truth and have a struggle with it, and at some point or other it begins to identify itself with the whole of the truth. You know, you'd die for it. Truth in the sense we're using it now includes those truths, to be sure. But truth in the sense of the aim of a human being is rather a different matter.

I'd rather not talk about it much more. There is a doctrine, that the truth is the object of the intellect, and the proper object of the intellect, and that in it you find all the other parts of a man.

It isn't just an intellectual matter, in the special sense of intellectual. This has to do with emotions and sentiments and love and the whole thing. The truth in that sense is a commanding thing, and an inclusive thing, pervasive, and you're always looking for it.

WOFFORD: Where does tragedy come in? You tie it entirely to little truths, particular truths?

BUCHANAN: I don't think it goes with the big one.

WOFFORD: Could you specify? Do you see any tragic recognitions that you've had?

BUCHANAN: No. I've never claimed I've been a tragic hero—I mean even to myself. I've never thought of myself that way. You kind of wish for it once in a while, but it's a pretty vain wish, and a pretty dangerous one.

WOFFORD: Don't you inevitably look both through the tragic and the comic lens?

BUCHANAN: Yes. Perhaps because it doesn't seem to go with my character completely, I think I've had more experiences with the comic than I've had with the tragic. Although some people would say no, you're melodramatic. Walter Stuart, who was a teacher at Amherst and a curious moralist, never approved of me. And the last time I saw him at Princeton, he was telling me again about myself, that I had always been looking for a cause and couldn't live without one, and that this was very bad. He was very serious about this. He liked me in a certain way, but he and a lot of people feel this way about my actions. I suppose this is what I've complained about, too—that is, that modern man is neither tragic nor comic, he's melodramatic.

WOFFORD: That's what Hutchins implicitly accused you of when he said that your vision of a giant Socrates coming out of the younger generation is the most wildly optimistic thing he has ever heard.

BUCHANAN: Well it was claiming a good deal. Standing all alone, it does sound romantic.

WOFFORD: You said your father's last words to you were "Are you going to be a doctor?" Do you have any current thoughts on doctors now that you're even more entangled with them?

BUCHANAN: I've always had ideas about doctors. Medicine's always fascinated me. I feel I missed something in not becoming a doctor. I might have done very well at it, not necessarily in the modern, scientific sense, but in what a physician is. I think I have the makings of that. I might have gone to town.

WOFFORD: It would have been particularly interesting if you had been a psychoanalyst. What remarkable fantasies you would have blown up!

BUCHANAN: Yes. When I was working for the Josiah Macy Jr. Foundation, the doctor who was the head of the Foundation was watching me, apparently because one time when I came back from Hopkins and told him what I thought of the philosophy of medicine, and that I was convinced I ought to be psychoanalyzed and take up that whole branch of medicine because it would be the modern philosophical framework for medicine, he looked at me and said, "Oh! I was afraid this was going to happen to you!" I never found out why he disapproved of it.

WOFFORD: Do you remember what you said to Schickele about immortality?

BUCHANAN: I don't remember very much of it.

WOFFORD: That's one of the Christian concepts I find most alien to me.

BUCHANAN: Me too—never interested me very much. It did at one moment; I guess I should own up to that. Just after I graduated from college I remember writing an essay just for myself. It wasn't very good, but it was an attempt to think through something. It wasn't real Christian immortality, it was more the kind of thing humanists would think of, influence on other people and that kind of notion.

WOFFORD: If time isn't in the picture, whatever happens, it seems to me, happens forever—if you're out of time, by definition, it's eternal.

BUCHANAN: That's right.

WOFFORD: This is what makes Father Hesburgh suspect I'm incorrigibly a Hindu.

BUCHANAN: Could be. I come very close here—I am horrified at coming so close to the Socratic view, sentimentally very close to what he says in the *Apology* and *Phaedo* about his long sleep or withdrawal from the conversation. I'll settle for either one. It doesn't make very much difference. It's a funny topic. You know, many Christians think that Easter is the greatest Christian holiday or feast and I've never agreed with this.

WOFFORD: That's my problem too. Good Friday and Christmas are my days. Easter is overlaid with stuff.

BUCHANAN: Overstuffed, that's a good word for it: overstuffed. All the talk about meeting old friends, former wives and husbands—damned nonsense, awful.

WOFFORD: Well, this is about a reel of tape. That's one way to measure a conversation.

BUCHANAN: That's right. You kept my breath going pretty well most of the time.

WOFFORD: Then maybe you ought to do something like this every day.

BUCHANAN: It might be good for my emphysema.

WOFFORD: You didn't have great trouble, did you?

BUCHANAN: Once or twice I was getting a little winded.

VII

THE
TWENTIETH CENTURY
SEARCH

[March 17, 1968]
with
Stringfellow Barr

Warm Bodies and Great Books

BARR: Scott hasn't come yet?

WOFFORD: This is his birthday, I hear. How old is he?

BARR: This makes him 73.

WOFFORD: Isn't this a hell of a birthday present, trying to put a conversation on tape and film?*

BARR: He's always humorous about his birthdays.

WOFFORD: You've trusted Scott on the most important things in a most remarkable way for about fifty years.

BARR: That's right. This trust business is pretty important to any educational enterprise. We're so afraid that as members of a democracy we'll have some kind of master-pupil relationship that is too parental or something, but if you don't trust the person you are trying to learn from, better not try. You'd better shop around until you find somebody you think you can trust.

---

*Buchanan and Barr agreed to let David Schickele film the conversation from which these excerpts are taken. The film version is available from the Center for the Study of Democratic Institutions, Santa Barbara, California.

WOFFORD: That's one of the best cases for the great books: that a lot of people have found over time that these are fairly trustworthy things. In recruiting a faculty now for a new college, when I am fairly low on finding human material, I at least can imagine that you have fifty or a hundred or a hundred and fifty teachers that you can get fairly cheaply.

BARR: And that it has taken about twenty five hundred years to produce. You remember my acquaintance at Old Westbury who wanted to know why I wouldn't rather learn face-to-face instead of with a book, and I objected that some of the people I knew best and liked most had been dead for a couple of thousand years and I was unwilling to give them up in order to be eyeball to eyeball, belly to belly, with people who happen to have warm bodies.

WOFFORD: One of the questions is whether Plato and Marx and all those in between have warm bodies—whether they come through speaking to you now. They did to me right after World War II at the University of Chicago, and when you design an education system, I discover, you keep wanting to inflict upon others your own best experiences.

BARR: You have none others to inflict, have you? If you assume that the crisis in our culture, which is deep, is so deep that we can learn nothing from the past, God help us. When a civilization reaches that point—America has always been near the point—of not being able to learn from the past, it's really had it. To put this many people on the same planet with no memory—it's probably better to turn it over to other animals.

(Buchanan arrives)

BUCHANAN: Harris, what is this you are doing with Bobby Kennedy?

WOFFORD: As he said in announcing his candidacy, helping him save the soul of the country.

BUCHANAN: Is it worth saving?

BARR: Can he save his own?

BUCHANAN: He trembled a bit when he said "soul."

WOFFORD: Do you remember the story of Radhakrishnan's encounter with Stalin. After touring Russia, the Indian president and philosopher told Stalin he had been impressed by many things, but Stalin sensed Radhakrishnan was holding something back.

"Did you find something missing," Stalin asked.

"Yes," said Radhakrishnan, "the soul."

"What is this thing called soul?" said Stalin.

"That which you have not got," said Radhakrishnan.

Is this Socratic knowledge, or do you have better knowledge of this thing called soul?

BUCHANAN: No, it's hard to talk about, though presidential candidates are doing it. The soul is a very volatile and complicated reflecting mechanism, so when you talk about it you're changing it. It holds a very funny place in human nature. It's an old philosophical problem. Radhakrishnan was just letting Stalin know he was not understanding it very well.

WOFFORD: Are we engaged in a contradiction in Socratic terms: a film of a conversation? Marshall McLuhan says a film is one-way communication, not a dialogue.

BUCHANAN: Well, I've never believed the Chinese proverb. I don't think a picture is worth a thousand or ten thousand words.

WOFFORD: Tell me about that notorious St. John's seminar about a kiss.

BUCHANAN: The question was: Is a sentence understood more intimate than a kiss?

WOFFORD: Any sentence?

BUCHANAN: Yes, *understood*.

BARR: I could imagine some women looking back on kisses and saying, "I believe you've got something."

WOFFORD: Scott claims my interviews have been very

intimate, and I claim that every time I touched an intimate button an idea came out.

BARR: He's never shrunk from intimacy.

WOFFORD: At the recent sessions here at the Center on the state of the soul of St. John's, 30 years after the New Program was started, I saw you perform a quite Socratic function for a current group of St. John's students. You stirred them—and perhaps irritated the faculty present—by saying that when you and Barr started the new program at St. John's, you didn't think that you had "the college" but that you had started a search. And you asked the current St. John's people, "How's the search going, and if it's still on, why do you have the same curriculum now that we had 30 years ago?"

BARR: Our program at St. John's was taken more as a declaration of war by academia than as a search.

BUCHANAN: The war was already going on, headed by Hutchins against John Dewey, but it's true it was a war. Anyone in the elective system is in a war always, a sort of guerrilla war, one against the other.

BARR: It would have been a war anyway, Scott, because just doing what we did was a very offensive critique of what colleges were doing.

BUCHANAN: Perhaps I ought to say a little more about the search—the search for a liberal college. We thought that we would perhaps discover something if we were actually teaching, as well as trying to think about liberal education, and in a curious way this was true right away at St. John's. We soon discovered, at least I did—I don't know how many other people did, not all certainly—that what we had at St. John's, although it was an almost complete structure, would never be anything more than a scaffolding within which you would hunt for the things you should be teaching and the ways to teach. A scaffolding set up to discover a building. In the middle of this scaffolding you would perhaps find that a part of it would become part of the permanent structure.

WOFFORD: What did you discover?

BUCHANAN: This is very difficult because the liberal arts change. Although in some sense the principle is the same, aimed at intellectuality, dealing with imagination and abstraction and that kind of thing, they pick up what is going on. For instance, right now the computers raise new questions about the liberal arts—very deep questions. In what sense do computers think? They do in one sense and they don't in another, but we are not sure about what that is. In order to pick that out you would have to find out what the liberal arts are today in terms of this distinction between the kind of thinking that computers do and the kind that men do, and then do something about teaching it. So if you found the institution of the liberal arts like a building, it wouldn't remain that way for any great length of time. It would be an institution that continually changes itself and reacts to the world around it. Where is thinking being done and how, is the main question. So to find the liberal college is to find the set of disciplines and questions, and to a certain extent solutions, but always on a continuing basis.

WOFFORD: Where do the great books come in? Our student planners at Old Westbury advised me to call them very good books.

BARR: Shakespeare is a very good writer.

WOFFORD: Are the great books the scaffolding in your metaphor?

BUCHANAN: Very much, it seems to me. There would be a core of them that would remain the same, but the list would change. This happened while we were at St. John's. There were certain books that we weren't sure of at all when we started but suddenly came into focus.

And vice versa, there were some we thought we knew a lot about but found very hard to teach. The great books themselves are a living thing. I see the figure of speech is misleading. Scaffolding is for a building. You wouldn't say that you have a central scaffolding for a human being. The thing you are after, to use another figure of speech, is an organ, a living organ, and the liberal arts are very much that if they are good.

BARR: One of the chief reasons for calling the very good books "great" is that they are apparently able to bring the intellectual process to life and have done so repeatedly in many historic contexts, although not in identical ways. They are in dialogue with every generation that wants to talk with them, since they talk much better than most books do. And that is why my friend Shakespeare is a great writer, not merely a nice one. Every time you go to a Shakespeare play you are amazed at how much you missed the last time you saw it. In the meantime you have had some experience that enables you to know what he is saying on this point. It is their power to multiply real dialectical relations between human minds that makes you keep coming back to more or less the same group of books.

WOFFORD: The most counter-revolutionary thing said about the St. John's program is that it is just right for about three thousand young people in this country and the problem is to find who those three thousand are. Are you saying the great books are for all people?

BARR: There are some people who haven't reached the point of being able to read them with as much understanding as some other people. But if they want to increase their understanding, I don't know a better place to go. We Americans have lost part of our heritage on this point. We know that some people we admire, for instance Abraham Lincoln, got rolling by reading things like Shakespeare or the English Bible.

WOFFORD: A very good book.

BARR: Yes, rather good. Yet people now almost seem to think: "How could you read the English Bible without first taking a course in Bible so that you would know what it was saying?" Through the centuries it has been a book, we ought to remember, God knows, that people who did manual labor have sort of thumbed through and painstakingly read and reflected on.

WOFFORD: The idea remains that the great books are for high I.Q. people and low I.Q. people can't take them. But the other day one of the men running a Yale program for ghetto kids said that he found, to his amazement, when he tried a very good though difficult book of Faulkner the students turned on far better, worked much harder, and got a lot more out of it than one of the simplified and so-called relevant books.

BUCHANAN: A really good book is very much more intelligible than a second-rate book. But you have to put in another thing: when people are reading great stuff constantly, they learn that even if they don't understand certain portions, if they keep reading they will. A child learns to talk by listening to people do it. You can do it even if at first you don't get it. And I know any number of people reading the great books who say I don't get anything out of it, I don't know what he is talking about—and then slowly it comes. It is like acquiring a foreign language. I am not at all surprised by your ghetto story.

WOFFORD: I had the same experience in Ethiopa. One of our Peace Corps teachers challenged me, "I dare you to come down and try teaching Plato to my twelfth grade class, to kids coming out of the *Mercato* (the market place)." I said, "Fine, I'll do the *Apology* and *Crito*." About a month later he came back and said, "You don't need to come. I tried it and it worked—it worked very well."

BARR: The view I get from a lot of young people is that these books are intellectual and they want something with emotion in it. The great books are packed with emotion. That is part of their greatness.

BUCHANAN: You may remember the original list from which the St. John's list comes, by way of Chicago and Columbia, was made up about 1885 for workmen's councils in England. These were labor union centers for miners and others. This was later picked up by a man at Columbia, a teacher of English that John Erskine had, and then Erskine used it, first for some American soldiers at the end of the first world war, and finally for the Honors course at Columbia. In a sense this was the only time when it was really snooty and aristocratic. We were using it in adult education in lower New York with very ordinary people.

BARR: And there was a very non-snooty use of it in public libraries around the country by the American Library Association.

WOFFORD: We have been considering an adult college in the midst of a regular undergraduate college. We would have older people coming to read great books and showing that, having tasted a lot of things, the thing they most want, they are most hungry for, is the stuff that would help them know the difference between a good and bad life.

BUCHANAN: A friend who had been in government for most of his life took me aside once at St. John's and said, "Your college ought to be set up for people fifty years old. That is when this would really count. We need wise old men, we haven't got any at the present and the world is suffering from this." And he would make them play football, too.

WOFFORD: Do you think it makes sense for us to try to get this process going with people who are out in action—in the ghetto or in Ethiopia or in a corporation?

BARR: One thing that troubles me about the education-in-action notion is, I hate to see a situation where people go to the books to get answers to questions they have already formulated. I think it is a misuse of a wise mind, and the minds of the people who wrote these books are wiser than most, to say, "I know what my problems are and I want you to give me solutions to them." Whereas actually the impact of these books is often that you never knew what your problems were.

WOFFORD: The son of a very dear friend committed suicide while he was a student at Harvard. A lively, fine, sensitive, very bright boy. I don't have any way of unraveling the mystery of it, but one of his student friends said, "We all feel we have to start completely on an open slate, to start from scratch and rethink everything—sex, politics, religion, everything. We have nothing to start with but ourselves, and that is a terrible burden." Part of the case for the great books is that you don't have to start everything over entirely.

BARR: One would hope not.

BUCHANAN: Although in another sense almost any parent knows this is true. His wisdom is almost no use to the next generation.

WOFFORD: That's one of our problems at Old Westbury. Some of us came in plying the great books, and the students saw this as authoritarian—the elders of the tribe passing on or imposing their tradition.

BUCHANAN: I don't really think there is much in this business of starting everything over again, in fact it is utterly fantastic—absurd. The relation of people to books is very complex, and seldom does any book impose itself on you in that way. You may live inside it in some way through imagination and so forth for a time. I've just been reading the life of Tolstoy and for about two weeks I couldn't get out of the atmosphere. It is kind of horrible as a matter of fact, but it wasn't imposing anything on me. Quite the contrary, I was getting over some kind of romantic attachment I have had to Tolstoy all my life—at least I was becoming aware of a lot of things. A book can do this. It may be pulling you to pieces—and making you rebuild what you had thought about something—but this frees you rather than compels you.

BARR: Frequently you react violently against a book the way you do toward your father.

BUCHANAN: And the violent reaction may be one of the finest things you can get out of it—real opposition.

BARR: What I object to is the idea that these books can't be really read unless you have a Ph.D. who tells you what they are saying. This is passing on or imposing a tradition in a way that I think ought to offend a young man living in a world of agony—this twentieth century world. But if on the other hand he is invited first to read the book, and the professor's chief obligation is to ask questions that may assist him to read it, this may get him in motion in relation to it. Then it's not a matter of getting the great book to tell him what to do in the twentieth century; it's getting him to think about the twentieth century and to see that the chaos in the world has another side to it—a side those of you who ran the Peace Corps ought to know, that for a great proportion of mankind this is not the century of collapse, but the century of hope.

WOFFORD: But many of the brightest and best of this generation, who see mainly chaos around them, say the great books represent an ordered tradition irrelevant to the twentieth century.

BARR: The great books are not cheerfully concerting to show you the world as neat. They are all quarrelling with each other—except that I think the argument is on a little better level than the bits and pieces of the current argument that I pick up.

BUCHANAN: Of course, Socratic teaching has nothing to do with the classroom or with books. Socrates was operating in the market place, or at least that's the expression for it usually. Apparently he spontaneously came on his method—as anyone might who was watching himself closely, and the questions were asked usually of ordinary persons who have opinions. The questioner is a kind of electric eel that shocks his listener into silence because he sees that he's silly.

Or take another figure of speech. There are births that are "wind eggs." They are empty births, and it's the business of the midwife to help with the delivery of this and then to test the product to see if it's a genuine baby, or whatever it might be, and you find some of them are fake. That is, they're false births and you get rid of the opinion that the person has given birth in this way. What's left, supposedly, would be some kind of an insight—at least a negative one: "That's not what I thought I thought." In that sense you are purging and getting rid of false foolishness and what you have left is some sort of wisdom.

Now this can be done with all sorts of conditions. The great books are an addition to it which may be dangerous as a matter of fact. I know there are occasions when the great book has been too heavy a lecture and you can't wake up a seminar afterward because it has done its indoctrination. But usually a great book doesn't have that effect. It is, rather, a conversation between a person and the book, and starts a conversation which can be encouraged and stimulated, carried on and continued under a series of questions.

Perhaps the book that seems to be the surest to produce a great conversation almost anytime, anywhere, with almost any people, is the *Oedipus Rex*. But why? Why it should be that kind of a book, I don't know. I know it's an interesting book—endlessly interesting to me—but just what about it produces such a good seminar I don't know. It's a good tragedy, as Aristotle said, probably the best one—and that ought to do this. But the process, the Socratic process, whatever it is—and it's a very complex thing—I don't suppose anyone fully understands.

WOFFORD: If you were giving advice to a young man today, what would be your advice on his education?

BUCHANAN: You mean where to go to college—that kind of question?

WOFFORD: If that's the kind of advice you give. How can a young man learn how to deal with his century?

BUCHANAN: Not to polish an apple, but I'd say go to some place that wants to be experimental.

WOFFORD: What would be the dangers you would warn him of?

BUCHANAN: That most places that are experimental are not worth going to.

BARR: An experimental college is a magnet to the discontented, and there are many reasons for men to be discontented—some of them very poor reasons. So you get constantly besieged by phonies. It was purple hell to get anybody that could teach the new program at St. John's. You must have had the same problem.

BUCHANAN: There is one thing we did not do that we set out to do, that is, to produce a new faculty out of our own students. We used to claim that within ten or twenty years we would have a largely alumni faculty. We supposed they would be better than we were. We thought of ourselves as lopsided and badly educated people, but those we were bringing up would be on the road to good things and some of them would be good teachers.

BARR: Whereas the people you could bring in would generally also be lopsided and badly educated. Now, according to Riesman and Jencks in their book *The*

188

Academic Revolution, the problem is all solved. It rejoices them that professors have become movable parts. If I don't like the way you treat me, I've got an offer from Stanford and I'll go where I am better treated. These Ph.D.'s are now, thank God—they seem to be saying—a highly professionalized group, although the picture they draw of their behavior shows more the racket side of the guild than the professional. For instance, they don't want to teach too much—they want to investigate. If this profession really wanted badly to teach in order to create or to help other minds to become investigative, I'd see a profession. But, in Riesman's picture they are an intellectual bureaucracy, a mandarin class who now are rather well paid—they used to be very badly paid—and who don't particularly want to teach. They want a light teaching load so they can publish and they want to publish because they are promoted for it. Riesman's not ashamed to say that.

Perhaps his tongue is in his cheek, but if so it's a very small tongue—his cheek didn't protrude—and he was at no point saying, What is the purpose of the college? He gives all the structure of the University, but it is like a picture of the Church that leaves out God. It is a sociology of the Academy, like a sociology of the Church. He seems to think it is quite a triumph that the professional scholar has taken over power, and now you can move any associate professor to any campus, not to yours maybe or to St. John's, but to practically any.

We couldn't do that, of course, and I hope you can't. We had no well to draw water from. We had to pick people that seemed to be discontented and unhappy for the right reasons, and then give them a chance to repair the damage.

BUCHANAN: It's a general problem for American education at present. Teachers are no longer teaching and we've got a second generation of this—people who don't even remember what it was to be taught.

WOFFORD: What do you mean by teaching?

BUCHANAN: A good deal. Whatever these people mean by it when they say they don't want to do it.

BARR: That's not quite true, Scott, because some of these people who don't want to teach mean they don't want to do the absurd things that are now being done in the classroom in the name of teaching. I don't want to do it either.

BUCHANAN: That's true.

BARR: What's wrong with so many academics is that they don't want to accept responsibility for inciting younger persons to use their intellects and to use them in such a way as to acquire intellectual habits that will free their powers to think better—to think more imaginatively and more rigorously and more sensitively. This assignment, I gather, doesn't really interest them. Therefore, in a funny sense you've got statistically more teachers than the country has ever had, and in another sense hardly any. There are some such people, but I think they are to be found much more in preparatory schools than in colleges.

BUCHANAN: There are a few everywhere, I suppose, but on the whole it isn't the habit of the profession anymore to do this, and they don't expect it of themselves and they don't expect people to learn that way. What's taken the place is information.

Chaos and Revolution

WOFFORD: You were born in 1895—and this is your 73rd birthday. That means the twentieth century has been within your scope ever since you began to remember anything. Do you see it steady and whole?

BUCHANAN: No, certainly not. But I want to see some order in it. I can't understand young people seeing chaos and wanting more of it. This is what puzzles me about them. The more chaos I see, the more I want order.

WOFFORD: So the twentieth century search is to discover the order in it, if it's there?

BUCHANAN: It would be for me, yes. The chaos is overwhelming. We're communicating less and less between human beings. Take even the discussion of great books. I think it's much more difficult to do than it was thirty years ago. Now this doesn't make me want to join the chaos. In fact, it's heartbreaking to see this.

WOFFORD: It made you want to make some of us in our law firm about ten years ago spend a winter reading Toynbee with you.

BUCHANAN: I remember.

WOFFORD: Is Toynbee a great book?

BUCHANAN: I don't know. It certainly is a very powerful and important book right now.

BARR: And very relevant.

BUCHANAN: Very important for America. Ten years ago I thought Toynbee had written for Americans. I still think he did. He was here recently and talked to us that way. It's a heroic thing he tried to do, but whether he accomplished it I don't know. I don't think he thinks so. You know, it breaks in the middle.

WOFFORD: Is his a tragic pattern?

BUCHANAN: Oh, yes, he thinks history is always a tragic pattern. This is where I joined him first enthusiastically. He sees the rise and fall of civilizations—the 21 or 26 of them, whichever way you count them—as tragic. But then after the first six volumes were written, before World War II, even he couldn't carry on that pattern. Civilization is no longer for him an intelligible unit of historical study. It breaks down like nations do, under his treatment, and he finally finds himself talking about the higher religions.

WOFFORD: Toynbee seems to be disagreeing with your proposition that the great object now is the world—not God, not man, but somehow the world.

BUCHANAN: I'm not sure I meet Toynbee on this. I suspect he wouldn't agree with my point, which is made in the conversation between Alyosha and Ivan in *The Brothers Karamazov*. Ivan, who's about to sell himself to the devil—or possibly has already—is reporting to Alyosha, a monk, that he has no trouble believing in God—that's easy enough. He finds it very difficult to believe in the world. He then goes into a catalog of horrors that he sees in the world: cruelty to children, oppression of workers, and all this kind of thing— a most eloquent passage. In some way this is characteristic of all of us at present. That is, God is not the real problem. He's there alright, although he may be dead at the moment, or hidden around the corner somewhere. But we are having just an awful time getting any steady view of the world or accepting it in more than a fraction of its parts.

We are living in a very special time, perhaps the most important time in history. One of the marks of this is that a great deal has happened in the last generation and the students are acting like Socrates and saying, "I know that I don't know," and asking everybody what they know and finding that they don't know either. And finally they've come to the point where they're getting other people to say they don't know. That means they are ready to learn—everybody—the young and older people, too. I may be wrong, but it seems to me true that more people today are claiming not to know and are asking questions in order to learn. The students, a very small minority, have been performing a very Socratic function for the rest of society—and all over the world, not just in this country. This is a very important time for that reason.

WOFFORD: Do you see this Socratic process connected inevitably with tragedy? Is it when you are caught in a tragic period that you find the breaking out of the learning spirit?

BUCHANAN: I wouldn't connect too closely Socratic questioning and tragedy, although, of course, any deep tragic hero at some point or other is doing this.

BARR: Reading the riddle!

BUCHANAN: Maybe even at the start of the action he may be working under a riddle of the Sphinx or some Delphic oracle or something. Put it another way, to use a very modern phrase—he's looking for his own identity in all that is going on, and this can be a tragic theme, to find out who you are.

WOFFORD: Is the true fate of a liberal artist then to be a tragic hero?

BUCHANAN: Either that or a comic hero—if he's successful. Most people are not—they are merely melodramatic. But it is in the liberal artist to think that way. Take Shakespeare's Hamlet. We think that he was crazy or he was melancholy or he couldn't make decisions, but actually if you read the play a certain way, he is asking all the relevant questions about his situation and this ends in a tragedy of a sort. In that way—though we are overusing the Socratic thing and suffering a good deal from it—Hamlet was asking Socratic questions of the situation all the time.

WOFFORD: You in your career, and St. John's in its manner and in its program, have asked for this Socratic trouble. You always seem to put Socrates at the heart of everything. Won't you admit to being a Platonist?

BUCHANAN: No. I don't know of any particular theory that Plato discovered or constructed or preached to anybody. All of his material was current in the Athenian

193

mind or in the Greek world at that time, and about the only novelty is Socrates. What Socrates did with all this material makes all the difference, but it doesn't add a doctrine to it. I realize that Plato's compilation of the Greek mind and passing it on is a source of practically all European thought. Everything since has been just a footnote to Plato, as Whitehead puts it.

BARR: Socrates once said, there is not much I know, but I do know one thing—that it's better to inquire than not to, and for this I will always stand ready to fight with my mind and my fists.

WOFFORD: When you were teaching at Fisk in the 1950's you showed this fighting side of Socrates to students who were then on the eve of the Negro revolution in the South. As I recall, they said it was very dangerous stuff you were asking them to do.

BUCHANAN: I wasn't asking them to do anything. It was their reading of Socrates, and I observed, sometimes very vividly, that they were hating Socrates or fearing him. We used to discuss this sometimes in class, but one occasion about three of them came around and spent the afternoon with me having this out and we got to talking about the purpose of the university and everything. I quoted Whitehead that "the university is the place to stretch young men's imaginations," and said Plato was asking them to do this. Socrates was, of course, a great trial for them. They thought their imaginations were being stretched a little too much, that I was a little unaware of what I was talking about. They said, "Let us tell you what would happen if we followed Socrates," and they described some of the things that were happening to Negroes when they acted that way. They were shot at and some of them killed. They were letting me know that this was a terrible thing for them, and they were having none of it at the moment. They weren't about to enter the revolution—but they did, as you know, a few years after.

WOFFORD: One of the problems is that so many enter the revolutions or great actions without getting their imaginations stretched or letting their imaginations be stretched, and that is a terrible thing, too.

BUCHANAN: It is.

WOFFORD: That's part of the case for finding a way to do this stretching in the midst of action. Gandhi tried it—the Peace Corps didn't try it very well.

BUCHANAN: Your emphasis on doing it simultaneously is what puzzles me.

WOFFORD: It isn't simultaneous if you spend an evening in a seminar, though you may have just come in from teaching in a ghetto school.

BARR: For Toynbee that would be an awfully fast "withdrawal and return."

BUCHANAN: It seems to me that's mixing things too quickly to give each one the effect it should have.

BARR: I can make a case for an education-in-action program today. The generation entering college has been deprived, largely by national affluence, of coming into contact with practical problems. They are a consumer generation and getting everything in containers and bottles and so on; and Scott's and my generation and to a lesser extent the generation that entered St. John's 30 years ago had had various experiences, maybe mostly in the summer because of having more time available, at being in the world. That is, once a year for three months we went back to the world in some sense—the world of very low practical problems. Now I can see how this generation feels hung-up by having had all of those problems solved for them. Put this together with the emergent world community which didn't exist then in the sense that it does now, I can see why you're saying, to sit down and read anything—no matter how powerful or great or important—without some immersion in practical poverty or whatever is unreal. A mean way to state it is that the generation entering college has lived, by the canons of mankind over many centuries, extremely artificial lives. Now, can reading correct that or do you not have to seek out some other devices?

BUCHANAN: You aren't saying that work is the only way that you get involved in thinking, are you? This is an old Dewey argument, that the only thing that will make a book interesting is having a practical problem.

WOFFORD: I deny that.

BUCHANAN: Good, I'm glad you do, and I would add that I would expect you to.

WOFFORD: But I don't get the case for saying the period of action should be without the Socratic element.

BARR: I'm more interested in making the case, particularly for Americans, that reading a book is not the time to say, "I believe that can help me Thursday night." That way you ask the wrong question of the books—the old American question, "What's this going to do for me?" I don't mean profit personally, but "What's that truth going to do for my life?" Well, for one thing it would give you a little squidget of truth which as a man you want and need. I think on the whole the American means, "Well, if it has no immediate bearing on my practical action, why are you bothering me? There is a lot of truth in the world, but I don't want that." In some way, any truth thus becomes only means, and this I object to. This is like saying, "I'll say my prayers if you can give me any assurance that God will give me what I ask for, because I want a thousand dollars." It is hard to imagine prayers that are not directed to something one already wanted, but to helping one find out what was worth wanting. This attitude is the heaviest baggage we carry. "Ivory tower" is the most hated phrase in American education, which causes me to suspect it is the one thing most needed—withdrawal long enough to reflect.

WOFFORD: The danger of education-in-action is that the time for education will be very brief and action will always be very seductive?

BARR: It may be like the promise to pray for one minute every day.

WOFFORD: I'm not so sure. Some people may come out of action, let's say teaching in a ghetto, ready for quite a few years of study or philosophy, I think we're going to be surprised by the effects of such student involvement. I can't yet predict the results, but the hope, the central educational strategy for such work-study programs, is the fact that the problems of the revolutions in the world—all the revolutions, including universal liberal education—are so complex that the students and faculty who are engaged in them are going to come back not seeking technical answers but stirred to get some theories and some ideas to deal with them.

BUCHANAN: That's a legitimate hope.

WOFFORD: When you started St. John's it was a kind of revolution, and in these last years you have been looking at the world revolutions. Do you see any connection? That is, can the revolutions in the world be made central objects of understanding in a liberal education today?

BUCHANAN: Since I'm strong for politics being a central theme in some sense, and most of politics in this period and probably for a long time in the future will be connected with revolutions, I suppose, yes, we have got to find a way of making revolutions reveal what they should to us. That will first call for a new version of the liberal arts that would enable students to grasp it. That will be very tough going.

BARR: Very tough for the young. Young men make excellent mathematicians and on the whole don't make excellent statesmen. Statesmanship necessarily involves a lot of experience.

BUCHANAN: Understanding revolution may be even harder for us old fellows in a different sense.

WOFFORD: Young men tend to see revolutions as comic and happy.

BARR: I don't know whether those who are involved in a real revolution see it in that way. The current youth revolt has a certain gaiety about it, but I don't think the nature of revolutions is gay.

BUCHANAN: It's more romantic than comic, isn't it? I mean a high romance that ends in great disillusionment.

WOFFORD: Instead of disillusionment you would have us see some tragic light?

BUCHANAN: Well, as the ordinary politician would say, try to see some realism in it. And that would involve disappointment—expecting disappointment.

BARR: And having the guts to go ahead though you expect disappointment.

BUCHANAN: Yes, some understanding of just what goes on, it needn't be any high doctrine.

BARR: Revolutions happen to be desperately disillusioning normally. Everyone that I recall.

BUCHANAN: Almost all of them to a certain point. This makes a great many people say that revolutions are either impossible or very undesirable.

BARR: It doesn't follow.

BUCHANAN: It doesn't follow at all, no.

WOFFORD: Would you state what you think is the nature of the revolution in the world today, if there is a central one?

BUCHANAN: No, I don't have any particular news about that. We hear all sorts of things, but it seems to me that the essence of a revolution is injustice and justice. Without reaching to that principle, or those principles, we are not understanding revolution at all. For the most part, people don't use those words about revolutions any more. They're out of fashion and out of mind to a great extent.

BARR: Negro speakers have been using them.

BUCHANAN: They were the only ones who were talking this way, yes. This was more true five years ago than it is right now.

BARR: They knew enough injustice in their own lives to think about justice.

BUCHANAN: You begin with merely knowing an injustice, you couldn't define it, you don't know what to do about it, but you're going to say no to it.

Reason - The Action of a Man

BUCHANAN: Reason and the life of reason, as George Santayana used to call it—where is it and how does it operate and what does it mean to us? Of course, I think of the intellect or reason (you can call it either thing) as *the* human trait, *the* human property—so that philosophy or the exercise of reason is *the* action of a *man*. His essence is involved in it, and anything that doesn't have reason in it is not very human, and anything that does have reason in it comprehends and informs all of his life, his feelings, even his physiological processes.

As I see it, reason penetrates the universe. It's in everything. I don't know of anything that isn't reasonable in its own mode. These modes are quite different for us. That is, the way it exists in human beings is one thing, the way it exists in one of these monarch butterflies is quite another thing, and in a rock or in a mountain still a different way, but they meet. The only explanation of human knowledge is that somehow

199

these things are identical. When you think a certain rational way you are thinking about something real.

WOFFORD: I am not sure I understand. You made me think of natural law. Law is said to be our "second reason." There are natural laws that are physical laws, and natural laws that have to do with human relations, and this puts the monarch butterfly and the human being in the same category. Is this what you mean?

BUCHANAN: Yes, because I am using reason without those qualifications. There is so-called natural reason and natural law and there is also human reason and human law, if you want to put it that way, but I am talking about reason in a very generic and general sense. It's the connection of those things that makes knowledge possible. I know you get taught in the philosophy classes and in a good many other ways at present that, of course, you mustn't confuse these things. That is, natural law is *only* concerned with human beings, and nature or the laws of science are quite different. That's true but they both have reason in them, and it's the recognition of this that makes all knowledge possible. And if I am right about the other part of this, that reason in a human being touches everything—his feelings as well as his thoughts and what are more generally called rational things—this is true of the part of man that is often called irrational. That is, there's reason in him in another way in his feelings.

WOFFORD: You just wrote a booklet, *So Reason Can Rule,* that suggests that the United States Constitution is committed to this proposition, and Justice Douglas wrote to you and said if you'd just gotten your hands dirty in the real law and the real Constitution, you'd see that this isn't what happens.

BUCHANAN: Yes, I'm trying to think of a short answer to Justice Douglas because his letter is very short and ought to be answered briefly. I haven't found the right sentence for it yet but I think there is an answer. I purposely wrote that piece so that it wouldn't get dirty. I wanted to say what the Constitution intended, not the way it actually works. It's a case of the lawyer baiting the philosopher and I want to turn it around and bait the lawyer—and say that if he didn't have his hands so dirty he might be able to understand what I was saying a little better.

WOFFORD: Or what the Constitution was saying?

BUCHANAN: Yes—that's more important, not what I was saying. I remember when Alex Meiklejohn and Felix Frankfurter had their arguments about free speech, something like this took place. Frankfurter said, "If I had my way I would send you to law school for three years," and Alex said, "If I had my way I would send you to philosophy school for four years." But it is pretty clear, although not many people recognize it now, the Constitution was written by men who were very much aware of this theory of reason and human nature. It is full of that language and of those assumptions. You see, the separation of powers in the Constitution—legislative, executive and judicial—are separable and recognizable things in human beings—in any human being's thinking. That is, you deliberate, you decide and then you turn around and judge it in a critical sense, and these powers in the Constitution fit that, and if you mix them up you get some pretty dangerous results. This is recognizing the great society as being a kind of macrocosm of the small society that exists in one's own mind, one's own soul. This goes along with Plato's *Republic*.

WOFFORD: I guess I am asking for your short answer to those who see chaos everywhere. The life of reason seems to be tragic. Whether it's our conversation or a seminar or anything that seeks the blinding light of reason, most of the time it's disappointing, deeply sometimes. If you look around the world, if you look at the United States Constitution, if you look at the federalism that was supposed to have persuasion as its principle, it's tragically defeated on most fronts.

BUCHANAN: Well, the life of reason is episodic, that is, it has little careers—sometimes they are very long. There are long periods in history in which they run very high and maintain themselves pretty well, but for the most part reason has only periods, or epochs, in which it is clearly operating.

WOFFORD: You are talking now about a person or about the body politic?

BUCHANAN: Both. It is true for a person's life and it's true for a society's life—in different ways again. Reason exists differently in a society than it does in the individual, but it is still reason. And the curve or the profile of these episodes is a tragic line; it may have comic traits too. In fact, not very often can an individual maintain that, but there have been lives and societies that do it over a short period. That's when the great dramas are written and sometimes the style spreads and the people live that way.

The story about the tragic end, of course, is not merely calamity and chaos, it's out of calamity and chaos that you get a recognition, a piece of learning, and that is perhaps the highest function of these dramas. You know in Aristotle's *Poetics* the end of a tragedy is the purgation of the emotions and the chaos and everything else, around the recognition. Sometimes it is a very profound recognition, sometimes a fairly simple one, but it's very important for the dramatic line—like Oedipus recognizing who he is, his father's son, whom he's murdered. This is a kind of ending for a tragedy which has become very classic, and people now identify tragedy with a calamity. But actually it should be identified with the recognition, what he learned by this. The point about recognition is symbolized in the *Oedipus* very strongly by a symbolic act. He puts out his eye so that he can see.

Want some more? The tragic blindness and the recognition scenes are the great parts of tragedy and the fact that there's a calamity and sometimes death ends it, is an accidental thing about tragedy, although you might expect such things to happen.

WOFFORD: A question the questioners of our college and yours ask, is whether what you mean by liberal education is in some sense the kind of freedom that, in the *Brothers Karamazov,* Ivan attacks in the name of the Grand Inquisitor. It is a freedom that carries with it a lot of pain for everybody, and unbearable pain for some. I suspect that at the heart of the stuff Winkie was criticizing in Riesman's book is Riesman's feeling that you have to tailor different kinds of education for different kinds of people—for the same reason that the Grand Inquisitor said the church had to put miracle, mystery and authority in place of freedom, in order to give happiness to most people.

BUCHANAN: It seems to me in this world at present there's no promise of happiness to many people. Happiness would be the life of a hero, and I mean this in the very real sense of a hero—not just one who becomes famous, but a person who's willing to pay the price for a certain kind of integrity and rationality and honesty, and he probably won't be very happy in the ordinary sense. He may be very happy in the extraordinary sense. That is, he's maintained his soul. He still has it whole. I think that's the answer here. I don't think you can square the good life today with superficial happiness. I'm sure you don't mean that. It hasn't been that way in my life, nor very much for anybody. Almost the opposite. There's a high correlation between superficial happiness and skullduggery.

WOFFORD: But Riesman's question to me has been whether in stretching students' imaginations, in the Peace Corps or in college—and since I like to have it happen to me I keep trying to make it happen for others—we are not stretching many people beyond the breaking point.

BUCHANAN: Probably you are. You have to face that. We used to say at St. John's that we were preparing people to be misfits, and we meant that in a very broad sense. Perhaps misfits in the universe for the time being. This is strong and some would say very cruel doctrine: ascetic and very puritan. But I think the world at present is asking for something like that. You can't get along without it certainly, not for any long time. If there's any of it left in the world, it better be preserved and brought into action.

I think that's it—thank you.

IMAGO MUNDI

[A Commencement Speech, St. John's College, 1952]

by Scott Buchanan

As you well know there is only one commencement
speech. It has been delivered many times and it has
many superficial variations, but it always says the same
thing. An old man of the tribe tells the young men that
they are beautiful and strong, that the world is full of
evils, and that they must go out into the world to fight its
evils and to keep the vision of its highest good. These
are the sentimental instruments of the great rite of initiation of the young into the tribe, but in spite of the
sentiment it must be clear that the great object that is
being celebrated is the world, and that the appropriation
of this object by each generation is necessary if it is
to live out its life.

The dogma that goes with this ritual is full of irony,
full of questions for seminar discussion, and I wish that
my part in your ritual could be less one-sided. Perhaps
the briefest statement of the dogma comes from F. H.
Bradley: This is the best of all possible worlds, but
everything in it is a necessary evil. But the irony is more
subtle than that and the questions are more complex.
A better statement says that the world does not exist,
it is merely an idea, but an idea that insists on being
entertained, and, once entertained, forces the mind to
believe that the world exists as the most real being. In
a few minutes today I want to try to contribute to your
celebration by initiating you as liberal artists to the
exploration of the idea of the world.

Dogmas, such as this one, are best stated as myths,
and this dogma is usually presented in a myth of creation. Here is a new one for this occasion. When God

created the angels, the brightest angel, Lucifer, immediately suggested that God create a world for him to govern. This disturbing suggestion delayed the work of the Six Days by making it necessary to create a Hell for all liberal artists who are too bright, and it also made God think twice before he created man. God finally resolved the problem by his delicate decision to give man an intellect which would have to reach for the idea of the world, but which would never comprehend it. The consequence is that Satan is never quite sure that he got what he asked for, and man has to learn over and over again that he cannot attain self-government unless he thinks and acts like an angel or a devil.

But perhaps we should begin with the simple, familiar illustrations and go on gradually to the bigger questions. Mark Van Doren in his book, *Shakespeare*, adds a point to Aristotle's *Poetics*. Aristotle says that poetry imitates human action, but by the use of the Greek word for poetry, the art of poetry, he presupposed that the poet makes something, something artificial, that can imitate action. If we ask what that something is, Mark Van Doren, in a tone of voice that leads one to suppose that he is saying something that everybody knows, says that the poet makes a world. This was startling when I first heard it from the lecture platform here at the College, but when I read it in the book I found it both disturbing and illuminating. I began thinking about it, particularly when I read a poem, but also when I began looking at the world in the framework of World Government. As a reader of poetry I found there was a world in a poem, not only in the great poems, but also in the little ones; but as an advocate of the devil in the Foundation for World Government, I found that a world was always something in a poem.

Out of Van Doren's suggestion and my own perverse philosophical habits I have come to an analysis of this addendum to Aristotle. The form in the poet's mind is an idea; it has unity, and a structure; it is a system, rather like a living system, it lives and moves. Furthermore, it is self-subsistent, a self-sufficient whole, needing and depending on nothing outside itself. Still further, having this kind of substantial existence and perfection, it is good, an object of love, a kind of Galatea to the poet's Pygmalion. It attracts and assimilates the poet so that his words become oracles, and the reader is attracted until he can no longer prevent a kind of self-immolation; he lives and moves in this veritable world. So it must have been when God created the world, and saw that it was good.

But then I realized that I was suffering a reminiscence, a recollection of the divine animal in Plato's *Timaeus*, which in turn had demanded an explication, an upward and downward dialectic. Plato's poetic intuition of his world, with its skeleton of being, non-being, same, and other, had been a preamble to his long discursive construction of the sciences, mathematics, astronomy, physics, chemistry, biology, and medicine. So there had been many poetic preambles to the sciences in the minds of poets turned scientists, or scientists turned poets. Lucretius, seeing the drift of his atoms and watching his Roman spearman testing the ramparts of the universe by eternally throwing his spear across the boundaries of space; Gilbert supplying Kepler with the magnetic parts of the celestial motor; Newton trusting that God's sensorium would be an adequate coordinator of gravitational pushes and pulls; and above all Dante and Kepler whose cosmologies of intelligence and love kept the planets in their courses; these were makers and knowers of worlds. It would seem that the eye of the poet travels out from the central intuition along the rays of light that the sciences provide to their vanishing points on the boundaries of the cosmos. The result of

this total vision, so many times repeated and so various-
ly formulated is the persistently recurring dogma that
the microcosm of man's mind mirrors the macrocosm
of the universe, that the human intellect is the place
of the forms, most of all, the place of the form of the
world. It is the business of a man to view with ever-in-
creasing awe the starry heavens above and the moral
law within.

This doctrine, once formulated and propagated by
its own overwhelming charm, has had a most profound
influence on the theoretical and practical affairs of our
civilization. It has impregnated every incipient science
with a hunger for wholeness and totality. Every abstract
proposition seeks, like a wandering orphan, for its place
in some deductive or demonstrative series, and the independent self-evident axioms of ancient contemplation
reduce themselves to postulates of systems that pretend
to comprehend the universe, just as cities grow into
metropolises and nations into mother countries in order
to preside over empires.

But there are signs that Satan has played his part
in these works of speculation and conquest. As the
universe of discourse tries to extend its boundaries, it
finds itself full of imitating and expanding systems, each
pretending to complete worldhood, and the more it
impresses the One on the Many, the more it spawns
new possible worlds, until discourse loses itself in an
infinite anarchical many. The principle of imitation,
which operated first in the poetic creation of a world
as an imitation of the small by the great, operates here
in reverse; the little systems imitate the great cosmos
without internal restraint or external restriction. Sometimes the great universe keeps a semblance of order
as in the concentric spheres of the Aristotelian cosmology, or as in the medieval cascade of analogies which
connects two systems of circles in Heaven and Hell with

a spiral purgatory; more often the universe reminds us of The Tower of Babel.

The modern world has for several centuries been spinning around us a new set of concentric spheres. They are not only crystalline, they also have high reflecting powers; they do it with mirrors. There is the system of gravity which impresses and diverts all particles from their inertial ways; there is the system of heat that releases by discreet degrees the random motions of sub-particles or molecules; there is the system of electro-magnetism that keeps all atoms and sub-atoms vibrating on all-pervasive waves of energy; and we now look, dazzled by these flashing mirrors, to find the new sphere of nuclear energy, which could be, we think, the unifying source of all our visions. But it may be well to remember Satan's challenge to God, and recall that the temptation to new creation is still continuing.

We did not need to be told some years ago that the universe is expanding, nor just yesterday that the re-creative process is still going on in interstellar space. We have been imitating the imitators in more intimate ways. We have built gadgets that can transform energy from one sphere to another, heat to mechanical equivalents, electricity to light, heat, and power, and tomorrow atomic energy perhaps to life. Under the aspect of the world, these gadgets have become a system of technology, which in its turn accelerates and expands the spheres of economics and politics, affairs of ours that have also become systems and systems of systems. If we listen to the biologists, the anthropologists, and the geographers, we learn that they have drawn loci for other reflecting spheres to control the light of the world. It would seem that by the principle of imitation and reflection we are living in a world that is bursting with a dozen possible worlds, each preventing the realization of the one world that our cosmic intellects require.

But if we draw a little closer and view the world with a somewhat more analytic eye, we shall see that this Satan-ridden machinery is not yet the tragedy that it seems. Worlds and systems of the kind we have been considering, like empires and governments, have come and gone in our intellectual history. The tragedies have all turned into comedies, as soon as worlds, systems and ideologies have been placed in the intellectual firmament. They are not principles nor are they facts, although they borrow something from both of these. They are hypotheses, and for all their heroic dimensions, and their high and mighty poses, they are only possibilities, which with boldness, laughter and ingenuity on our part can be put aside and replaced. None of them has the sufficient reason that is needed to give it actuality. The best of all possible worlds is yet to be found, if Satan is to be confounded and God is to be justified.

We listen to the poet because he offers us a possible view of the world, and both he and we are ready to be fooled by the imposters, because we have great need of a view of the world. In that sense possible worlds are necessary if we are ever to find our actual world. But there are several demands that the possible world never fulfills, demands that a possible world cannot by itself fulfill. An actual world has to be all there is; as Plato showed in the *Sophist*, an actual world has to contain even non-being. It turns out on examination that a possible world is always too big and at the same time too little to be a real world. It is not merely, as Kant would say, that a possible world leaps beyond experience; it easily goes beyond all possible evidence, and just at this point begins to fabricate its own evidence, its own self-subsistence. We see this imitative creation on a grand scale at present with the help of the spectroscope, the Palomar telescope, and the cosmotron. Lucretius's spearman was a very modest fellow beside these modern mechanics who draw geodesics with a ray of light.

But it is also true that a possible world is too little to be real. The poet, turned scientist and philosopher, being finite, leaves a great deal out of his vision; at the beginning he does this by arbitrary intention and then continues to do so on principle. If he falls in love with his Galatea, we know that the course of his love will not be smooth and that he will awake from his trance, knowing that there are more things in heaven and earth than he has dreamed of. A possible world is radically abstract and only parades in the habits of a world historic character.

Perhaps I should stop here and let you go out into the world armed with the comic spirit of the critical philosophy. But this is where Kant stopped and rather irresponsibly let the world set sail in the eighteenth century, not dreaming in his philosophy of half the things that would happen in its voyage through the nineteenth and twentieth centuries. But he left word that the idea of the world was an irreplaceable idea of reason, which although it led to speculative monsters which must be avoided, still guided the searching mind in its worldly work, and furthermore defined a duty for the individual to act on maxims that are laws iniversal, that is to say, world laws. And as a sanction for this last bit of moral advice he said something that sounds like the detonation of the big bomb: you can choose the peace of the grave, or the world state.

So the world, as an idea of reason, is not merely a fool's fable, not merely one of many possible worlds. If we allow our minds their speculative indulgence, even to the limit of a Satanic multiplication of such worlds, a heavy duty is laid upon the practical intellect to weigh these worlds, to choose the best of them . . . and to will it. Although Leibniz trusted God to supply the sufficient reason to make this choice, there is a strong presumption that some of God's powers were delegated to man, and that among these powers are those of just government derived from the consent of the governed. It seems that the founding fathers of this country accepted this responsibility, to consider all possible worlds, to choose the best, and to will it. "It has been frequently remarked that it seems to have been reserved to the people of this country, by their conduct and example, to decide the important question, whether societies of men are really capable or not of establishing good government from reflection and choice, or whether they are forever destined to depend for their constitutions on accident and force. If there be any truth in the remark, the crisis at which we have arrived may with propriety be regarded as the era in which that decision is to be made; and a wrong election on the part we shall act, may, in this view, deserve to be considered as the general misfortune of mankind." The idea of the world in its practical imperative form was pressing hard on the minds of the authors of the Federalist Papers when this statement was written. It is pressing still more heavily on all our minds today.

It would require a new Virgil with his pious Aeneus to weigh the burden that the idea of the world has put upon us, and to distribute the weight among us so that it can be carried. We have something like such an Aeneid in Arnold Toynbee's *A Study of History,* which I am persuaded was written for twentieth century Americans. As you know, he focuses his enormous working knowledge of the world upon those stages in civilization which, remembering Greek tragedy, he names "times of troubles." The troubles arise chiefly from the accumulation of unsolved problems and from the pervasive ambiguities in the situation. Toynbee describes these times of trouble in some twenty past civilizations, and

212

then heightens the irony in ours by describing it as the locus of simultaneous confluence of the five or six civilizations still extant and in process of breakdown. Toynbee lacks the liberal artist's disciplined appetite for the broad general and abstract conceptions that lead from poetry and science to the idea of the world. He therefore sees the welter of cosmologies and utopias as the pathological content of the schism in the individual soul which suffers progressive separation from its neighbors and the community. Incidentally he sees our science, technology, economics, and politics as systems of deadly radiation that emanate from the still vital centers of Western civilization to the rest of the world. In this he is of course guilty of the cosmological disease himself, seeing himself as the head physician in a pathological clinic with the world as his patient; he would be the last to deny this observation.

I would not like to dispute his pessimistic prognosis, but its depth might be increased by a bolder and more objective consideration of the cosmic content of the pathological symptoms. If Kant and Plato are right that it is a man's duty to view all time and eternity, and this not merely in the historical mode, cosmology is a normal, even necessary, human preoccupation. In times of stress it may be that the cosmos runs a fever and shows other monstrous symptoms, but medicine has always known that many symptoms of disease are the appearances of the process of natural healing or even of recovery itself. At any rate the liberal artist, who has to have the final judgment on medical matters, may have something to add to pathology.

Toynbee would not deny that in the midst of death there is birth, as the world goes, and with a new world there will be need of a new world view. Wendell Willkie some years ago made himself the herald of a new world, which he called One World. Soon after we find ourselves needing to accustom ourselves to Two Worlds, the East and the West, as they are defined in ideological terms. One has only to go to the Middle East, or almost anywhere else, to find that the idea of two worlds has indeed taken root, but the two worlds are not the same that Americans and Russians see. This is the idea of the world playing its old game of dividing and multiplying by the rule of two, with Satan joining in by proposing the Third or Middle factor. From the point of the view of the divine world-animal it is the delegation and redistribution of powers. Each situation is a problem in measurement and redefinition. In this view it is not surprising that there are paroxysms of mutual negation, veto, and deadly conflict, in some cases pacts of mutual suicide. Toynbee would say that there is danger of the vast process grinding human communities and individuals down to dust so that the particles can be fitted into one vast universal state. But the sense of panmixia, or promiscuity and abandon, and the opposite reaction of asceticism in the individual need not be signs of immediate dissolution. They could be signs of the first new impact of the idea of the world, and a waiting readiness on the part of the recipients to accept the measurement and redefinition that it promises. One of the impressive functions of the cosmic idea is to preside over the birth of possible, new, and good worlds, and to incite new wills to make them actual. Willing abandon, promiscuity, and asceticism are sometimes signs of grace.

There are many signs at present that measurement and redefinition are taking place. The instruments of precision and the terms of definition often buckle and fracture under the heavy pressures to which they are subject, but the world principle creates others to take their place, and finds new occasions for their operation. It is said that American influence at present radiates

on beams of science, technology, economics, and politics, and that it is the reverse echoing beams from the
rest of the world that frighten us. For instance our
confusion of science and technology leaves us as prag-
matism, and Russia sends it back as dialectical materi-
alism. Our confusion of economics and politics leaves
us as corporation law and returns to us as the Soviet
Republic. The scramble that ensues to get positions of
strength makes us aware that the rest of the world needs
and wants these gadgets but that they will find new
utilities for them that we have not even imagined, and
may not be able to understand until we have invented
new possible worlds to fit them.

There are signs in this country that we have forgotten
a great deal of the political science from which our own
government was constructed. We seem to think that a
good government, once established, waxes strong and
continues established forever unless it is destroyed from
without. It should therefore be defended both externally
and internally to preserve its way of life. But if it has
a political life, we must remember the lesson in the
eighth book of Plato's *Republic* in which the world view
of government sees a political beginning, middle, and
end; with good luck an aristocratic philosophical birth,
a youth of timocratic or military rule, a good plutocratic
middle age under oligarchs, and a second childhood
of democracy and tyranny—perhaps a rebirth, if all these
possible worlds have been fulfilled faithfully. But even
in our obstinate American way of life we are learning,
not only that governments are born in philosophy and
blood, suffer concentrations of power, and then indulge
in high standards of living, but that any government,
if only to defend itself, has to limit and adjust itself
to other governments, so that each state is potentially
and increasingly actually a province of a world state
which federally defines and conditions the operation of

the local laws. We now know from hard experience that international law, which governs unilateral relations of individual states with their neighbors, presupposes a world law which philosophers have from time to time vainly proposed, sometimes to conquerors who have used the idea for their own worldly purposes. A deeper thing we have learned is that this world law, like the idea of the world, has to deal with all possible legal systems. The world contains all sorts of governments today, and the problem of jurisprudence is to find the transformation formula which will rationalize the political relativity that now nags us with its apparent whimsies of local times and places.

But one of Plato's political categories seems in the last century to have sprouted a new monster. It is customary in a seminar to translate oligarchy into plutocracy under an ancient formula that the concentration of political power in a few hands follows the transfer of property from the many to the few. This formula has a very modern radical sound even when it is a mere footnote in the reading of a great book, and it is fitting that it draws this attention because it is at this point that the monster has grown, the modern welfare state, in which the world of trade and industry and the science of economics touch public political interest in vital ways. The changed nature of war in which industry plays a greater part than mere armaments, and the meaning we have recently given to security, beyond the limits of mere defense, these are signs that the economic systems which permeate the world are more than invisible governments, and that they must be recognized as subject to political growth. But as we see this, it also becomes clear that there are many economies, some of them never before recognized as economies, such as the feudal estate, from which capitalism and socialism have come historically. But again these systems do not merely

216

show a life history of a single kind of economy, but rather a contemporary mosaic of economic systems, none of which has ever existed separately or purely, but always together, like governments, in essential co-operation and conflict with each other.

The science of economics came into existence as a byproduct of capitalism. Under the pressure of socialistic theory it has had to defend itself from the charge of being the science of scarcity and imperialism. From unsuccessful attempts to plan national economies it has now been forced to survey world economy, just to keep its predictions of the local market from too great errors. It is now clear that the theory of economic imperialism, like the theory of international law, is merely the first hypothesis that leads to a cosmological development within which the relativity of economic systems will act as the epicyclical components of a great economic cycle, which is not, by the way, to be confused with the business cycle, or so we hope. The economic intercourse between feudal, capitalistic, and socialistic economies is apparently unavoidable as a political concern, although the proper study of corporations as the mediums of this intercourse might show that giant national corporations are not the only competent sovereigns.

All this might be the airiest exploration of possible worlds if it were not for the ground swell of science and technology that has been built up by two world wars, and propagated like a tidal wave of revolution all over the world. It is now common knowledge in the farthest corners of the world that hunger, sickness, nakedness, and homelessness, all those symptoms of the economy of scarcity under which we have all lived, can by the proper multiplication and distribution of science and technology be abolished from the earth. This is not something that can be brought to pass tomorrow nor in the next decade; neither is it merely the demagogic sentiment of a political orator. Science and technology themselves have gone far enough in their own estimates of themselves, under the inspiration of the idea of the world, to measure and redefine the possibilities. Through all the sound and fury of the United Nations, this is what the still small voices of the FAO and ECO-SOC are saying, and little, hungry, sick, naked, homeless people everywhere are listening. This knowledge is rapidly transforming itself into the general will of the world and expressing itself in many revolutions. In spite of the surface phenomena of acceleration in the economic system of this country, the real industrial revolution has gone underground, and is now sprouting everywhere; it is no wonder that the face of the world wears a troubled look. This possible world needs God's as well as man's will to make it actual. But the stirrings of men's wills are at present expressed only in emotions of fear. We are not sure what our gadgets, planted all over the world, will do to us; we need a technological cosmology to quiet our nerves and to guide the conduct of our public affairs. If this view of the present world is at all valid, there is a remarkable enticement to reconsider Kant's proposal of the moral ideal of the world, the categorical imperative, in its three forms. He proposed it just as his contemporary, Adam Smith, was drawing in the first outlines of the industrial revolution and trying to estimate its effect on the wealth and welfare of nations. Kant was trying to foresee the common reasonable legal forms under which nations and economies would assimilate the progressive developments in science and technology. The necessary conditions for such laws were equal powers of legislation and equal rights for all human beings; the conception of each person as an end in himself, not a means only; and finally the conception of the whole natural world under men, as a kingdom of ends. Having stated these conditions as absolutely necessary moral principles, as if to confess his failure of imagination, he called them merely ideals, things that we must will but cannot hope to fulfill. This is the way they have been presented in courses in the history of philosophy for almost two hundred years. At long last we have come to see that they are ideals that must be fulfilled if any part of the world that we know and love is to survive. We are now convinced that we must make another try, that it is our duty to hope. Laws must be made that are just for all men; economies must be made for all men, and not men for economies; and the means of science and technology must be made available for universal use. What we know we can do, we must do. The rotation of the spheres, beginning with the sphere of mechanics, then shifting to the sphere of heat, then to the sphere of electricity, has finally actuated a sphere of technology, and therefore the spheres of economics and government, and this has put a massive substance into the pure form of the categorical imperative.

But Kant's great questions still remain: What can I know, what can I hope for, what ought I to do? The idea of the world, coming to us through this imminently realized form of the categorical imperative has us thoroughly frightened. It has particularly frightened us Americans, because the world has passed to us the primary responsibility for carrying out the duty, and we appear to have the primary means. But this is not the first time that the idea of the world has frightened human beings; the ideal has often turned into a menacing fate over which mere men seem to have no control. This is the phenomenon that is being diagnosed in Toynbee's pathology. He is describing the quasi-world of men as the receptacle for the idea, and to the lonely individual the world of men seems to have broken into fragments, and he looks around for another receptacle that can adequately take its place. Until he finds this, his consent is paralyzed. The individual in very un-Socratic manner thinks he knows nothing, and waits for fate to tell him what he can hope for and what he ought to do. I think there is a great general will in the world that will finally articulate and answer these questions, but it will take a long time for this idea of the world to express itself in individual minds.

I am going to take the liberty of acting temporarily as your class prophet. When I graduated from college, as I remember, we voted for Lewis Douglas as the man most likely to succeed, but we did not specify the category of his success. I shall try a more actuarial method, specifying categories and suggesting probable frequencies of your answers to the Kantian questions.

Some of you, probably the larger portion, will want to forget the infinity of possible worlds, even the best possible, and decide to cultivate your suburban gardens. As you know, you will have eminent philosophical authority for your decision, and realizing this, you may want to re-read some of the great books to choose your style of garden, the Epicurean, or possibly a Stoic porch. I hope you will acquire the comic spirit because I am afraid you will not be left alone and undisturbed; your protecting hedge will have to be a stout sense of humor. A few others of you will smell adventure in a wide open world and your curiosity will lead you to explore all the possible worlds that you can get passports to. You may be frightened by the monsters that you meet, and also by those that you will help create, but you will escape all of them, one after another, and find that each world through which you pass will be a university, a university of trial and error with the degree, Bachelor of Experience.

Some of you, who have come to St. John's looking for a philosophy of life, will by this time have fallen in love with an actual world of the recent or distant past. You will not realize that a past actual world, although it was once possible, is now an impossible world, and you will seek to defend it with your life. You may leave an island for some Sancho Panza to govern and after many battles against evil find your Dulcinea and your final victory in heaven.

Still others, I presume a very few, will be bored with the cobwebs and dreams of the books of the past, with the State Department and the Un-American Activities Committees of the present, and will find your only escape in the future. You will think it your duty to smash this sorry scheme of things entirely into bits from which you will be willing to build the only really possible world, the city of the future. You may remember that Aristophanes wrote his *Birds* about you, and realize that you are probably already a citizen of a city not built with hands.

The rest of you, if there are any left, will, I take it, become citizens of the world. You must already know that it is a feverish, impatient world, not very tolerant of any full exercise of the liberal arts, especially those that contemplate alternative possibilities, not generous or sympathetic with those who find it necessary to measure and redefine their loyalties. You may find any simple loyalty you have suddenly cancelling other loyalties that you wish to keep, and you may be charged with many treasons within the hour. You will find the words you use and the deeds you do marvellously ambiguous. All these things will be so because you have made the idea of the world the rule of your life, you have found a way of accepting the actual world, and of accepting the fate that it contains as the necessary condition for solving your problems. This may mean that you see the need for a world government or a universal church, as Toynbee suggests, but it more probably will mean that you will want to see that the laws that you live under are made truly universal and the God you serve less like an idol. It should lead you to see that the persons with whom you work are not merely useful but with you serve common ends, that the parts of nature that you exploit are made useful to your fellows as well, that the science and skill that you have is made available through education to everybody.

These simple sounding truths were accepted by the founding fathers of this country; they have regularly been accepted in the Western world; and they are now being accepted by all of the rest of the world. They are all rules of world law. They with the possible worlds that they comprehend and permeate are making the world revolution which will probably continue through the rest of your lives.

Perhaps the most important thing that the contemporary cosmopolitan, the present citizen of the world, has to remember is that the world lives and moves, it revolves, and that revolution is its natural property. The sudden and explosive phenomena, that we often call revolutions, are epicyclical rotations or mere perturbations, often retrograde, mere symptoms of the deeper and larger work of the world, the rattling and wobbling of the wheels of the great chariot. If you are sensitive, imaginative, and responsive, these agitations will disturb your feelings and your wishes, but your reason will say with Galileo: Still it moves, and your will will consent.

It may be that some of you will find that your consent has become a deep settled habit and sentiment, and that you will want to join your generation in its acceptance of one of the most characteristic expressions of the idea of the world in a time of troubles, that is, the almost universal movement of peoples. Tolstoy describes one such episode in *War and Peace;* General Smuts and Wendell Willkie refer to the present episode as "the people on the march." These movements usually start from the internal pressures and the external conquests of great wars and first appear as scattered and displaced persons, the victims of the malice that is generated by social frustration. But the movement quickly outruns the cause, becomes voluntary and self-directed on the part of both the proletariat and the intelligentsia. It falls into the pattern of willed possible worlds of many kinds. Finally it appears as the colonial spirit with the avowed pioneering purpose of resettling the world. As you know I have recently been temporarily participating in one stage of such a movement in Israel, one that bids fair to become the model for many others. Properly enough for the time we in this country and in Europe tend to see our part in the great movement as the development of backward areas, and to see the prospective colonies as appendages of one or another of the great empires. It is safe to say that these less-than-world-views will suffer revision, if only because imperialism is an outworn notion. The new view will see the new settlements as colonies of the world. Those of you who are attracted to the suburban garden, have a yen for adventure, and an appetite for revolution, but do not want to leave the world to indulge your private fancies may potentially belong to the new pioneering stock. If this be your beloved fate, we shall welcome you back to some class reunion to tell us what has been going on in the world. The final paradox that I will not now try to explain is that the light from the idea of the world is now shining on the world's periphery; it is we at the presumed center who live in darkness . . . and fear.

There are three words familiar in the Zionist tradition, *diaspora* or wandering, *kibbutz* or in-gathering, and *aliyah* or going-up; they indicate motions of the world. I could wish that they would make the pattern of your individual lives.

223

APPENDIX I

MEMORIAL MINUTES

1968-69 PROCEEDINGS
THE AMERICAN PHILOSOPHICAL ASSOCIATION

SCOTT BUCHANAN
[1895-1968]

Scott Buchanan died after a long illness on March 25, 1968, in Santa Barbara, California. He was born in Sprague, Washington, on March 17, 1895. He majored in Greek and Mathematics at Amherst College, where he received an A.B. in 1916. He taught Greek for a year at Amherst during the educational experiments and innovations of Alexander Meiklejohn, after which he served in the Navy during the first World War. He read philosophy at Balliol College, Oxford from 1919 to 1921 as a Rhodes Scholar. He continued his study of philosophy at Harvard University, received a Ph.D. in 1925, and taught during this period at Harvard and at City College in New York. From 1925 to 1929 he was Assistant Director of the People's Institute in New York, where he directed and planned programs in adult education. He was Professor of Philosophy at the University of Virginia from 1929 to 1936. He then went to the University of Chicago to organize and direct the Committee on the Liberal Arts. In 1937 he became Dean of St. John's College in Annapolis, Maryland, and contributed to the construction in one of the oldest colleges in America of a bold undergraduate program based on the Great Books and the Liberal Arts. He left St. John's in 1947 to become Director of Liberal Arts, Inc. of Pittsfield, Massachusetts, and later Consultant and Secretary of the Foundation for World Government. In 1956-7, he was Chairman of the Religion and Philosophy Department at Fisk University in Nashville, Tennessee. From 1957 to his death he served as Consultant and Fellow of the Center for the Study of Democratic Institutions in Santa Barbara.

Buchanan's writings are a record of a continuing analysis of the nature of philosophic insight and inquiry and of a ranging exploration of their applications in different fields and disciplines. In *Possibility,* published in 1927, he acknowledged an ambition to seek "a general methodology, not merely for this or that discipline, but rather an organon of intellectual imagination." He distinguished three kinds of possibility: imaginative possibility expressed in the fine arts and literature, scientific possibility elaborated in systematic concepts applicable to experience, and absolute possibility, expounded by philosophers and theologians; and he ordered his exploration of the realms of possibility on the assumption that our intellectual culture is constituted by a plurality of theoretic systems, each relatively opaque, but possessed of formal characteristics which are capable of mutual reference and of analysis into elements which can be stated abstractly and in isolation from the systems to which they belong. Much of his later work was an exploration of possible worlds and of the modes and consequences of their actualization.

The adult education program of the People's Institute was such an actualization in the American tradition of popular and general education. Buchanan organized and gave lectures on morals and politics and on natural and social science in the Great Hall of Cooper Union and smaller lectures and discussions at the Manhattan Trade School and the Muhlenburg Branch of the Public Library. In those meetings the liberal arts were rediscovered and re-examined and the Great Books were studied on the model of the General Honors Course newly established at Columbia University. A handbook on the Classics of the Western World was prepared by the teachers of the courses at Columbia and the People's Institute and was published by the American Library Association. In 1929 Buchanan published *Poetry and Mathematics,* based on one of his courses, in which he traced analogies and mutual reinforcements and supplementations found in the arts of language and of mathematics. *Poetry and Mathematics* was reissued in a paperback edition with a new Introduction in 1962. Buchanan found further suggestive indications concerning the nature of mathematics as a liberal art in the works of George and Mary Boole. Stimulated by George Boole's discussion, in the last chapter of *The Laws of Thought,* of the constitution of the human mind which is able to solve differential equations and generalize the method to all thought, he spent a year in England studying the works of the Cambridge mathematicians contemporary with Boole who called themselves the Analytic Society. In 1932 he published *Symbolic Distance in Relation to Analogy and Fiction.*

Medicine and architecture were liberal arts in Varro's list of nine liberal arts from which the seven medieval liberal arts were derived. In 1934, when the first rumblings of the coming of socialized medicine were heard in America, Buchanan was invited by the Josiah Macy, Jr. Foundation to explore the possibility of acquiring a philosophy of medicine for this country. He spent a year at the Johns Hopkins Medical School, attending classes in anatomy, physiology, biochemistry, and pathology, and working in association with the Institute in the History of Medicine under Dr. Henry Sigerist. He studied the relation of medicine to the theories of the modern sciences and the place of philosophy in the Hippocratic writings and in the works of Galen. In 1938 he published *The Doctrine of Signatures: a Defense of Theory in Medicine.*

From the beginning of his journey of rediscovery and revolution Scott Buchanan had related the evolution and the themes of the liberal arts to the history and the problems of politics, constitutions, and culture. In 1953 he published *Essays in Politics.* His services at the Center for the Study of Democratic Institutes were a continuing dialogue on politics and the liberal arts, some of them published as conversations or essays, many of them still in manuscript or on tape. In 1962 he published a Conversation *On Revolution,* in which he examined the tradition of revolution in the formation and interpretation of the American Constitution and urged the importance of legitimizing revolution. His last essay, published in March 1968, the month of his death, was "A Message to the Young," in which he relates the fundamental revolution of the world and of thought to particular, occasional, and disruptive revolutions: "Perhaps the most important thing the present citizen of the world has to remember is that the world lives and moves, it revolves; revolution, indeed, is its natural property. The sudden and explosive phenomena that we often call revolutions are mere symptoms of the deeper and larger work of the world, the rattling and wobbling of the wheels of the great chariot of time."

Scott Buchanan was a teacher and a learner, a man of doctrine and of discipline in the ancient senses of those two words. He adapted the themes and topics of the history of thought and action to the circumstances of concrete experiences and to the problems of present emergencies, andhe sought liberating arts and regulating disciplines to guide men in the specification and in the use of the possibilities of imagination and the ideas of wisdom.

RICHARD MCKEON
Distinguished Service Professor
of Greek and Philosophy,
University of Chicago

APPENDIX II

THE 1937-38 CATALOG
OF
ST. JOHN'S COLLEGE,
written largely by Scott Buchanan

[Facsimile]

THE NEW PROGRAM AT ST. JOHN'S COLLEGE

ST. JOHN'S COLLEGE is a small liberal arts college for men. It is non-denominational, and has been so since its founding. It has never been co-educational. It maintains no graduate or professional schools. It is the third oldest college in the United States.

Attention is focused upon it today because in September, 1937, a new College administration introduced the so-called "New Program," a four-year all-required curriculum, based on the study of some hundred great books from the Greeks to the present. The New Program is designed to furnish a sound general education. At St. John's it has replaced the elective system of numerous departmental courses which characterizes American colleges today. No other American college is offering a curriculum similar to the New Program.

St. John's College is deeply rooted in the American tradition. In 1696 the General Assembly of colonial Maryland passed the following Act:

CHAP. XVII

A Petitionary act for free-schools. Lib. LL. No. 2. fol. 115. Dread Sovereign . . . .

Being excited by his present Excellency *Francis Nicholson,* Esq.; your Majesty's Governor of this your Province, his Zeal for your Majesty's Service, pious Endeavors and generous Offers for the Propagation of Christianity and good Learning, herein we become humble Suitors to your most sacred Majesty, to extend your Royal Grace and Favour to us your Majesty's Subjects of this Province, represented in this your Majesty's General Assembly thereof, THAT IT MAY BE ENACTED,

II. AND MAY IT BE ENACTED, *by the King's most excellent majesty, by and with the advice, prayer and consent of this present General Assembly, and the authority of the same,* That for the propagation of the gospel, and the education of the youth of this province in good letters and manners, that a certain place or places, for a free-school, or place of study of Latin, Greek, writing, and the like, consisting of one master, one usher, and one writing-master, or scribe, to a school, and one hundred scholars, more or less, according to the ability of the said free-school, may be made, erected, founded, propagated and established under your royal patronage. And that the most reverend father in God, Thomas, by Divine Providence lord-archbishop of Canterbury, primate and metropolitan of all England, may be chancellor of the said school; and that, to perpetuate the memory of your majesty, it may be called King William's School, and managed by certain trustees, nominated, and appointed by your sacred majesty.

Laws of Maryland, Session of July 1-9, 1696.

"King William's School," established in accordance with this Act, flourished until the Revolution, when, according to tradition, its building became a gunshop. In 1784 the Legislature granted the charter for St. John's College; in the following year an Act was passed which transferred the masters, students, and funds of King William's School to St. John's. The College has, therefore, a tradition reaching back to the seventeenth century.

The "fundamental and inviolable principles" of the College charter are recognizably principles also of the Declaration of Independence. Indeed, one of the signers of that Declaration, William Paca, was among the petitioners for this very Charter; and three other signers, Charles Carroll of Carrollton, Samuel Chase, and Thomas Stone, served on the Board of Visitors and Governors of St. John's College.

But the founding fathers of St. John's and of our Republic were aware that the liberties they had won with blood could be lost through folly and inertia. To prevent that folly they determined that our youth should possess a liberal education and in the preamble of the College Charter they declared:

WHEREAS, Institutions for the liberal education of youth in the principles of virtue, knowledge and useful literature are of the highest benefit to society, in order to train up and perpetuate a succession of able and honest men for discharging the various offices and duties of life, both civil and religious, with usefulness and reputation, and such institutions of learning have accordingly been promoted and encouraged by the wisest and best regulated States:

Be it enacted, etc.

The founders of St. John's College and of similar colleges of liberal arts knew that, although *habeas corpus* can protect a free man's body from tyranny, only a liberal education can protect his mind. They even knew that, once the mind falls under the subtle tyranny of ignorance, grosser tyrannies soon flourish. They were therefore aware that "the wisest and best regulated States" strike at the roots of tyranny by establishing and maintaining liberal education. It was with such notions in mind that George Washington, who had visited St. John's, wrote its Faculty: "I sincerely hope the excellence of your seminary will be manifested in the morals and science of the youth who are favored with your care." Seven years later he sent his adopted son, George Washington Parke Custis, to St. John's College, which President Washington's nephews, Fairfax and Lawrence, had already attended. To the same generations of St. John's men belong Francis Scott Key, 1796, and Reverdy Johnson, 1811, later Minister to Great Britain.

A few decades ago, St. John's College, along with countless other American colleges, followed the lead of Harvard under President Eliot and introduced the "elective system," under which with increasingly few restrictions the student chose which subjects he would study and which he would not. During those decades, the many separate courses one took in order to secure a bachelor's degree became more and more specialized and less and less related until the American undergraduate wandered in a maze of scheduled "offerings," choosing those courses which were easiest or which were taught by men he liked or which came at a convenient hour of the morning or which seemed likely in some way to increase his chances of getting rich in later life. The curriculum at St. John's, like the curriculum of other American colleges, suffered this decay. But in 1937 the Board of Visitors and Governors of St. John's, recognizing this decay, turned for guidance to the Committee on the Liberal Arts, which President Robert Maynard Hutchins had set up at the University of Chicago for the purpose of investigating the proper content of a liberal arts curriculum. The result of their consultation was that four members of the Committee consented to undertake at St. John's a restoration of the liberal education which its Charter calls for. Of these four, Stringfellow Barr assumed the Presidency of the College, and Scott Buchanan became Dean of St. John's.

In September, 1937, the New Program was introduced, but it seemed wise for the first year to permit incoming freshmen to decide between the New Program and the Old Program or elective system. One-third chose the New. The remaining freshmen entered the Old Program, which was also followed in the three upper classes. A few upper-classmen sacrificed the "credits" towards a degree which they had acquired in the Old Program and entered the New Program as freshmen; for piecing together the two programs was not permitted. By January it was clear that the initial problems of organization had been met, and the Board of Visitors and Governors ruled that, beginning with September, 1938, the New Program should be the required curriculum for all students at St. John's except those who had already been admitted to the Old. It is for these that the present catalogue contains information relevant to the Old Program, for these and for students who may desire to transfer from other colleges to St. John's at the grade of sophomore or higher. On the other hand, students who enter St. John's as freshmen need concern themselves only with the requirements and content of the New Program, and the same thing is true of students who have studied at other colleges but who wish to enter as freshmen in the New Program. Except that certain New Program lectures are open to all members of the College, the two programs of study do not in any way overlap.

The student who proposes to attend a liberal college, whether St. John's or some other, will do well to consider first the aims of liberal education. Two or three generations ago, there would have been no point in discussing those aims in a college catalogue. They were implicit in the college curriculum. Today college catalogues rarely discuss the aims of liberal education, but for a different reason: in the minds of our generation they have become confused and obscure. Irrelevant aims have been substituted: social contacts, athletics, college activities, vocational training, preparation for money-making, merely satisfying minimum requirements for entrance into graduate and professional schools, the acquisition of pleasanter manners. Yet a liberal college is neither a club, nor a trade-school, nor a finishing school, nor an asylum for the young unemployed. At least, it ought never to consent to be these things. A liberal college should be concerned with supplying the student with a liberal education, and the student who considers entering a liberal college should know what the aims of liberal education are.

A scientific writer of the nineteenth century defined education as the adaptation of the human animal to his environment. Human animals, like other animals, have physical wants: they must, as we say, make a living. But, unlike other animals, human animals have intellectual and spiritual wants as well. Like other animals, human animals may be trained. Unlike other animals, they must be educated too, if they would be really human.

We Americans, in our eagerness to open and exploit a continent, have emphasized the practical, the utilitarian, the economic. We have practised brilliantly the useful arts. But, in doing so, we have rediscovered what our ancestors knew: that back of the practical lies theory, that true utility depends on distinguishing means from ends, that economic goods are the means to life but not its sufficient end. In pursuing the useful arts, we have been led back to the liberal arts: the arts of apprehending, understanding, and knowing. It was to teach these higher, and exclusively human, arts that our ancestors founded and endowed the "college of liberal arts." For they knew that it is only by practising the liberal arts, by understanding and knowing, that the human animal becomes a free man. It is only by discipline in these arts that spiritual, moral, and civil liberties can be achieved and preserved. No wonder the founders of St. John's College considered such arts "of the highest benefit to society"—more truly "useful" than a trade-school, useful as they knew trade-schools to be. But our ancestors knew likewise that, although the useful arts of making a living ultimately depend on the liberal arts of apprehending and understanding, the liberal arts are not best studied as a mere balance-wheel for the useful arts. Ultimately, the ends of liberal education are the intellectual virtues. The human animal does not desire knowledge merely in order to eat. He desires knowledge because he is human. The relation between the useful arts and the liberal arts, between "practical education" and what men have for centuries called a "liberal education," may be briefly stated if we remind ourselves that we eat to live but that we do not live to eat. To live, we must eat: we must therefore learn and practise the useful arts. To live as free men in a free society, we must also think, imagine, speculate, understand: we must therefore learn and practise the liberal arts if we would live responsibly and freely. For all who would live in this human fashion, not merely as animals or slaves, liberal education has therefore a high "utility," and colleges of liberal arts are "of the highest benefit to society."

The liberal arts are the arts of thinking, and we human animals think through symbols. The liberal arts are therefore the arts of handling symbols. Since the symbols through which we think are of two general sorts, words and numbers, it is not hard to see why for many centuries the liberal arts have been practised primarily on languages and mathematics. But the words we learned from our parents' lips, the language we think and speak in, the ideas which lie behind that language, all these represent a complex which we call tradition. If we understand that tradition, if we constantly expand and criticize it, we utilize the full heritage of civilized human animals. If we try to escape from tradition, to live without that heritage, we are doomed to live blind and uncivilized lives. If in our confusion we then try to concoct a synthetic tradition—and this has happened in our own days in many places—we become monstrous; and for the proper authority of tradition we substitute tyranny.

All men, including college freshmen, have traditions and live by them: local traditions, family traditions, even personal day-to-day traditions; professional traditions, scientific and literary traditions, political traditions like monarchy and democracy. But all these traditions are parts of the great liberal tradition of Europe and America, which for a period of two thousand years has kept watch over and guided all other Occidental traditions. The liberal college is concerned with transmitting this rich heritage and with continually restating it in fresh and contemporary terms. The tools which it requires, in order to do this well, are the liberal arts. The most tangible and available embodiments of the tradition itself are the classics.

The "classics" which liberal education made use of until recent decades were Greek, Latin, and mathematics. But it made increasingly bad use of them. It made, indeed, such bad use of them, that it eventually forgot why it had chosen them. In the circumstances, it began quite naturally to drop them out of the college curriculum. Unfortunately, it has never since succeeded in finding adequate substitutes, and its wild efforts to find such substitutes have resulted only in cluttering the college curriculum with tidbit courses in ill-related subject-matters. So conspicuous has this failure been that the college student long ago turned from his scheduled courses to athletics and other extra-curricular activities to find the discipline which the class-room no longer supplied. Curiously enough, at this point the college, recognizing that the courses it offered were educationally less successful than student activities, turned some of the activities into courses, in a vain effort to recapture control of the educational process. This is the unconscious origin of courses in journalism, public speaking, athletic coaching, current events, which characterize liberal colleges today.

Recognizing this series of failures in liberal education, a number of men in different university faculties set to work to find again the point at which the tradition of liberal education had been lost. This finding again, this "research," went on in many places for many years, but by separate paths eventually converged upon the great books of the European intellectual tradition. These great books are the medium in which our liberal heritage has been rediscovered, in which it can be revived, in which it can be taught again in the liberal college. In that sense the great books are still classics. In that sense too liberal education should still be classical.

Since the word classic has many meanings today—there are "the classics" of Greek and Latin literature, and there are boxing "classics" in the world of professional sport—this may be the place to state the standards by which one may judge a book to be a classic.

To begin with the apparently trivial, a great book is one that has been read by the largest number of persons. To followers of the publishers' announcements of best sellers this criterion may seem unworthy. Over the entire period of European history, Plato, Euclid, the Bible, and Shakespeare are the best examples: barring historical accidents, such as the burning of the library at Alexandria, the judgment stands. The second criterion is also apparently numerical: a great book has the largest number of possible interpretations. This does not mean that the book must be confusingly ambiguous; it rather refers to the inexhaustibility of its significance, each interpretation possessing a clarity and force that will allow other interpretations to stand by its side without confusion. Dante's *Divine Comedy* and Newton's *Principia* are the telling examples under this standard. The third criterion is more important and harder to determine: a great book should raise the persistent unanswerable questions about the great themes in European thought. Questions concerning number and measurement, matter and form, ultimate substance, tragedy, and God open up mysteries for the human mind. These questions are met and evaded regularly by self-styled practical men; faced and explored, they induce, balance, and maintain the intellectual virtues, and on their constant cultivation hang the issues of orthodoxy, heresy, and freedom which are always with us. The fourth criterion is that a great book must be a work of fine art; it must have an immediate intelligibility and style which will excite and discipline the ordinary mind by its form alone. Fifthly, a great book must be a masterpiece of the liberal arts. Its author must be a master of the arts of thought and imagination whose work has been faithful to the ends of these arts, the understanding and exposition of the truth. These five are the tests which a book must pass if it is to belong to any contemporary list of the classics.

But such a list makes a chronological series with an order that imposes additional powers on each book. Each book was written after and in the light of previous books; each book was written before other books which it has influenced. Each master has stood on the shoulders of another master and has had later masters as his students. These influences, which are historically vague in some cases, are impressive in the books themselves. Each is something more than itself in its organic place in the series, and this has many implications. One cannot internally understand a given book until he has read its predecessors and also its successors. It turns out that the best commentary on a great book is another great book. Books now unintelligible to both professor and student become approachable and conquerable if the proper path through other books is followed. Finally the educative value and power of any given book increases at a very high ratio as other books are read. Consider Euclid and Newton, Sophocles and Freud, Plato and Kant, Hegel and Marx, Locke and the American Constitution. This is an overwhelming answer to inevitable doubts whether the modern college student has capacities equal to the task of reading which the St. John's program sets. It is also internal evidence from the books themselves that they are the best instruments of education. Current textbooks in special subject-matters do not belong to the classics; they are the best examples we can find of books that are detached from the tradition and therefore doomed to early death.

Several models and a great deal of teaching and reading have gone into the compilation of the list. There is the experience with the American Expeditionary Force University at Beaune at the end of the War, there is the experience with honors courses at Columbia University during the twenties, there is the experience with adult reading courses in connection with the People's Institute and the New York Public Libraries, there is the experience with undergraduates, graduates, and high school students at the University of Chicago, there is the experience with Litterae Humaniores at Oxford, there is experience in the Benedictine monasteries from the sixth century on. But the best model that we have is the Bible, a series of books so selected and ordered that they have become the Scriptures of the whole race. This is the most read book in our list, and its inspiration has spread backward and forward through all the classics.

It should be added that any limited list of the classics must always remain open to revision. There is no better way of revising it than its continuous use in teaching in a college. The "best hundred books" is a variable for collecting the values that satisfy its criteria. That is the minimum way of describing the scholarly task that is laid on the teaching faculty.

The books on this list for the most part have recently been republished in cheap editions. The cost to the student during the four years' course will, with a few exceptions, come within the customary sum paid for textbooks. In special cases, for instance Euclid's *Elements* in Heath's translation, the College has arranged a subsidy. It is therefore feasible to make and remake such a list, and to prescribe it as the required reading of all students at St. John's who enter the new program of study.

THE LIBERAL ARTS

There are two ways of explaining the function of the liberal arts in a liberal college. The simpler way is to describe the mechanics of instruction. That will appear in what follows. But first it will be well to make clear what the basic distinctions were before the modern chaos buried them under the materials of instruction. In general the liberal arts are the three R's, reading, writing, and reckoning. So they still appear in our primary schools; it is their integrity and power that still lure us back to the little red school houses where our fathers

(*Continued on page 28*)

A LIST OF GREAT BOOKS

In Chronological Order

Homer: *Iliad* and *Odyssey*
Æschylus: *Oresteia*
Herodotus: *History*
Sophocles: *Œdipus Rex*
Hippocrates: Selections
Euripides: *Medea* and *Electra*
Thucydides: *History of the Peloponnesian Wars*
Aristophanes: *Frogs, Clouds, Birds*
Aristarchus: *On the Distance of the Sun and Moon*
Aristoxenus: *Harmony*
Plato: *Meno, Republic, Sophist*
Aristotle: *Organon* and *Poetics*
Archimedes: Works
Euclid: *Elements*
Apollonius: *Conics*
Lucian: *True History*
Plutarch: *Lives*
Lucretius: *On the Nature of Things*
Nicomachus: *Introduction to Arithmetic*
Ptolemy: *Almagest*
Virgil: *Æneid*
Strabo: *Geography*
Tacitus: *Histories*
Cicero: *De Officiis*
Horace: *Ars Poetica*
Ovid: *Metamorphoses*
Quintilian: *Institutes*
Marcus Aurelius: *To Himself*
The Bible
Galen: *On the Natural Faculties*
Plotinus: *Enneads*
Justinian: *Institutes*
Augustine: *De Musica* and *De Magistro*
Song of Roland
Volsunga Saga
Bonaventura: *On the Reduction of the Arts to Theology*
Thomas: *Summa Theologica*
Dante: *Divine Comedy*
Roger Bacon: *Opus Maius*
Chaucer: *Canterbury Tales*
Leonardo: Note-books
Erasmus: *Colloquies*
Rabelais: *Gargantua*
Copernicus: *De Revolutionibus*
Machiavelli: *The Prince*
Harvey: *On the Motion of the Heart*
Gilbert: *On the Magnet*
Kepler: *Epitome of Astronomy*
Galileo: *Two New Sciences*
Descartes: *Geometry*
Francis Bacon: *Novum Organum*
Hobbes: *Leviathan*
Montaigne: *Essays*
Cervantes: *Don Quixote*
Shakespeare: *Hamlet, King Lear*
Calvin: *Institutes*
Grotius: *The Law of War and Peace*
Corneille: *Le Cid*

Racine: *Phèdre*
Molière: *Tartuffe*
Spinoza: *Ethics*
Milton: *Paradise Lost*
Leibniz: Mathematical Papers
Newton: *Principia*
Lavoisier: *Elements of Chemistry*
Boyle: *Skeptical Chymist*
Montesquieu: *The Spirit of the Laws*
Swift: *Gulliver's Travels*
Locke: *Essay Concerning Human Understanding*
Voltaire: *Candide*
Fielding: *Tom Jones*
Rousseau: *Social Contract*
Adam Smith: *Wealth of Nations*
Hume: *Treatise of Human Nature*
Gibbon: *Decline and Fall of the Roman Empire*
Constitution of the United States
Federalist Papers
Kant: *Critique of Pure Reason*
Goethe: *Faust*
Hegel: *Science of Logic*
Schopenhauer: *The World as Will and Idea*
Coleridge: *Biographia Literaria*
Bentham: *Principles of Morals and of Legislation*
Malthus: *Essay on the Principles of Population*
Mill: *System of Logic*
Marx: *Capital*
Balzac: *Père Goriot*
Thackeray: *Henry Esmond*
Dickens: *David Copperfield*
Flaubert: *Madame Bovary*
Dostoevski: *Crime and Punishment*
Tolstoi: *War and Peace*
Zola: *Experimental Novel*
Ibsen: *The Doll's House*
Dalton: *A New System of Chemical Philosophy*
Clifford: *The Common Sense of the Exact Sciences*
Fourier: *Mathematical Analysis of Heat*
Faraday: *Experimental Researches into Electricity*
Peacock: Algebra
Lobachevski: *Theory of Parallels*
Darwin: *Origin of Species*
Mendel: Papers
Bernard: *Introduction to Experimental Medicine*
Galton: *Enquiries into the Human Mind and its Faculties*
Joule: Scientific Papers
Maxwell: *Electricity and Magnetism*
Gauss: Mathematical Papers
Galois: Mathematical Papers
Boole: *Laws of Thought*
Hamilton: *Quaternions*
Riemann: *The Hypotheses of Geometry*
Cantor: *Transfinite Numbers*
Virchow: *Cellular Pathology*
Poincaré: *Science and Hypothesis*
Hilbert: *Foundations of Geometry*
James: *Principles of Psychology*
Freud: *Papers on Hysteria*
Russell: *Principles of Mathematics*
Veblen and Young: *Projective Geometry*

and grandfathers studied and practised them. Before the nine-teenth century they had a higher place and a more elaborate development which gave birth to and nurtured the array of subject-matters in the modern university. For fifteen hundred years they were called the Seven Liberal Arts, and before that they were called the Encyclopedia, the "circle for the training of boys." There is a continuous tradition of these as there is of the books, and the two traditions are one in the end. Their formal and operating techniques are more difficult to recover than their products in the great books, but the recovery has proved possible and also illuminating for the practical problems of instruction that the books raise.

The clearest historic pattern of the liberal arts for the modern mind is, curiously enough, to be found in the thirteenth cen-tury. At the time of Dante's *Divine Comedy* and St. Thomas' *Summa Theologica,* they were listed as follows:

Trivium	*Quadrivium*
Grammar	Arithmetic
Rhetoric	Geometry
Logic	Music
	Astronomy

With the medieval emphasis on the rational activities of man and the central position of the speculative sciences of theology and philosophy interest centered on the last art in each column, and the other arts were subordinate and auxiliary to them. The master of arts in the thirteenth century would most likely write his books on logic and metaphysics or in music and astronomy. Other ages made different emphases. The Renaissance found rhetoric, geometry, and music (measurement) most productive and illuminating, with the other arts subsidiary. The Romans went farthest in rhetoric, as one might expect from noting their legal activities. The Alexandrians gave highest honors to the grammarian scholar and the arithmetician and geometer, with considerable consequent attention to experimental science. The Athenian Greeks agreed with the thirteenth century in their ordering of the arts. It seems that we in our political preoccu-pation and economic energy, coupled with experimental sci-ence, are primarily concerned with rhetoric and music, the Pythagorean name for mathematical physics.

The order and the shifts in order that this indicates reflect the shifts of attention and emphasis in the great books, and these in turn, as methods of writing and reading, may be said to reflect the spirit of the ages in which they were written. These observations are turned to account in the manner of teaching followed at St. John's. The entire period with the books and the patterns of the arts can be recapitulated in the four-year college course, the yearly divisions falling respectively at the end of the Alexandrian period, at the end of the middle ages, in the middle of the eighteenth century, and ending with contemporary writers. The schedule can be seen in the scheme on page 30.

This scheme correlates the books with the appropriate contemporaneous ordering of the liberal arts, and provides the basic pattern of instruction so that it will be most effective and economical. The two outside columns give the divisions of the books that are primarily literary and linguistic in medium and style and those that are mathematical and scientific in these respects. The middle column gives the texts that expound the distinctions and ordering principles of the arts of reading, understanding, and criticism that will most efficiently exploit the contents of the books. Along with these, laboratories of three kinds are successively used, one to study the devices of measurement and instruments of precision, another to repeat the crucial and canonical experiments in the history of science, and still another for the focusing and concentrating of the devices of all the sciences upon such contemporary problems as the nature of the cell, the chemical, physical, and biological balances in the blood, and the basic problems in embryology. These are the non-bookish classics that the modern laboratory has produced, and the consequent disciplines are provided for the liberal training of the student. It is an interesting fact of modern times that the classics and the liberal arts are kept alive chiefly by experimentation.

The liberal arts are chiefly concerned with the nature of the symbols, written, spoken, and constructed, in terms of which we rational animals find our way around in the material and cultural world in which we live. Symbols have practical aspects, as in rhetoric and industry, which must be understood and distinguished from their theoretical uses and significances in science and literature. Again there are concrete data and artificial pro-

SCHEDULE OF READINGS BY YEARS

	Languages and Literature	Liberal Arts	Mathematics and Science
First Year	Homer Herodotus Thucydides Æschylus Sophocles Euripides Aristophanes Plutarch Lucian	Plato Aristotle Lucretius	Hippocrates Euclid Nicomachus Aristarchus Apollonius Archimedes Aristoxenus
Second Year	Horace Ovid Tacitus Virgil The Bible Quintilian Dante Volsunga Saga Song of Roland Chaucer	Aurelius Cicero Plotinus Augustine Bonaventura Thomas Roger Bacon	Ptolemy Galen Leonardo Copernicus Galileo Descartes
Third Year	Cervantes Shakespeare Milton Rabelais Corneille Racine Molière Erasmus Montaigne Montesquieu Grotius	Calvin Spinoza Francis Bacon Hobbes Locke Hume	Kepler Harvey Gilbert Newton Leibniz Boyle
Fourth Year	Gibbon Voltaire Swift Goethe Rousseau Adam Smith American Constitution Federalist Papers Malthus Marx Fielding Zola Balzac Flaubert Thackeray Dickens Ibsen Dostoevski Tolstoi	Kant Schopenhauer Hegel Peacock Boole Bentham Clifford Mill James Freud Poincaré Hilbert Russell	Fourier Lavoisier Dalton Hamilton Faraday Maxwell Joule Darwin Virchow Bernard Galton Mendel Cantor Riemann Lobachevski Gauss Galois Veblen & Young

ducts that must be distinguished from the abstract principles and ideas which govern them. There are many connections that these aspects have with one another, and it is the business of the liberal artist to see these apart and put them together. Success in this constitutes intellectual and moral health. Failure is stupidity, intellectual and moral decay, and slavery, to escape which the founding fathers set up institutions of liberal education. It is reassuring to know that they had more than pious hopes in their minds when they made charters for St. John's College and its sister institutions.

Despite daily assertions to the contrary, there is no educational device for assuring worldly success to the student. To cultivate the rational human powers of the individual so that armed with the intellectual and moral virtues he may hope to meet and withstand the vicissitudes of outrageous fortune— that is education.

INSTRUCTION

The machinery of instruction adopted for the New Program was worked out step by step at various places during the past two decades, at Columbia University, at the University of Chicago, at the University of Virginia, and in connection with adult education carried on in New York City. It underwent further adaptation during the session 1937-38 at St. John's. It has been so devised as to furnish the student with a maximum of balanced training through a combination and rotation of teaching techniques. It is dictated by the books read and by the liberal arts.

The teaching devices in the New Program are four: (1) reading and discussion of the books in seminars; (2) formal lectures on special topics in the liberal arts; (3) tutorials; (4) laboratories.

SEMINARS

Meetings of seminar groups occur twice a week with any additional meetings that special circumstances or difficulties may indicate. There are at least two instructors in charge, and the instruction makes use of a wide range of devices from *explication de texte* to analysis of intellectual content and the dialectical treatment of critical opinion.

FORMAL LECTURES

The liberal arts operate in the light of principles which constitute the liberal sciences. These sciences are progressively expounded in formal lectures by various members of the staff as the course proceeds. The lectures are expository and critical also of themes that arise in the reading of the books. There are at least two formal lectures a week.

TUTORIALS

There are two kinds of tutorial instruction for small groups or individuals: in original languages and in mathematics.

The study of an original language is initiated in an intensive manner during a period of six or eight weeks at the beginning of each year. The books are read in English translation, but their proper interpretation is most rapid and efficient when they are studied as translations. This requires only a part of the knowledge commonly demanded now in language courses, a knowledge that is rapidly and easily acquired by the study and analysis of texts selected from the books on the list. This training serves three purposes in the course.

First, it contributes to a knowledge of universal or general grammar as that is studied in the liberal arts. Secondly, it develops in the student a cumulative skill in the reading of any text whether in a foreign language or in English. Third, language training at St. John's includes memorizing short passages, imitating the style of great writers, translating, and criticizing. These things are done in order to induce in the student an active participation in the thought of great authors, to increase his original literary ability, and to incite him to original literary creation. All these aims were formerly achieved through the study and thoughtful translation of Greek and Latin before our colleges first forgot why Greek and Latin had been chosen as educational mediums and then almost completely discarded them.

The second kind of tutorial is ordered to the elementary study of the mathematical books. Modern students, more because of the diversity in previous trainings rather than because of any genuine differences in native endowments, vary a great deal in their mathematical abilities. The mathematical tutorials are organized and taught on the basis of diagnoses of individual cases with the aim of leading each student into vital intellectual relations with the mathematical texts. This task is facilitated by the mathematical laboratory for those whose difficulties lie in the operational level.

LABORATORIES

Three kinds of laboratories are used: one in mathematics and measurement; one in experimentation; and one in the combination of scientific findings.

The mathematical laboratory is equipped with the basic instruments of measurement in all the sciences. Here students learn the mathematical principles that have been embodied in the instruments, learn to operate them, and thus become familiar with the operational aspects of both mathematics and the natural sciences. They also acquire the "feel" of elementary laboratory techniques for all the sciences.

The second kind of laboratory allows students to repeat the crucial and canonical experiments in historic and contemporary science. There are classics in empirical science, experiments which once uncovered principles and laid the foundation for whole fields of investigation. Some of these go back to the lever and the balance, some of them like Galileo's experiments with the inclined plane founded classical mechanics, others like Milikan's measurement of the force on the electron have set the themes for contemporary science. Students are familiarized with these scientific classics.

At the end of the course there will be a laboratory for the combining of scientific findings in order to investigate concrete problems of central importance. The best problems come from the medical sciences, problems of the cell, problems of blood balances, problems of embryology. They will be in charge of a member of the staff who is acquainted with medical science.

These laboratories provide a proper pre-professional scientific training, illustrate the liberal arts in their liveliest contemporary practices, and focus the past on the present for the whole course. The mathematical laboratory carries the student through the first year, the experimental laboratory through the second and third years, and the combinatorial laboratory through the last year.